AUTISM &

ADOLESCENCE

THE WAY I SEE IT

DR. TEMPLE
GRANDIN

What Teens and Adults

AUTISM & ADOLESCENCE: THE WAY I SEE IT

All marketing and publishing rights guaranteed to and reserved by:

FUTURE   HORIZONS

(817) 277-0727

(817) 277-2270 (fax)

info@fhautism.com

www.fhautism.com

ISBN: 978-1-957984-98-8

CONTENTS

CHAPTER TWO

CHAPTER THREE

CHAPTER FOUR

FOREWORD

BY TEMPLE GRANDIN

At age four, I had no speech, but I was lucky to receive really good speech therapy and early education. Today I am a distinguished professor of animal science at Colorado State University. Early childhood educational methods that are effective are discussed in my previous book *Autism and Education: The Way I See It*. I have been giving presentations about my experiences with autism for over forty years. There have been great improvements in early childhood programs.

A major stumbling block for many autistic individuals is making a successful transition to employment and independence. This book will help guide autistic individuals into employment and successful adulthood. Parents often underestimate an autistic child's ability to learn new things. There is often a tendency to overprotect and do too many tasks for their child. Many times, I have met fully verbal teenagers on the spectrum who are good at academics but have not learned life skills. They have never shopped in a store by themselves or ordered food in a restaurant or learned how to budget money.

Grandparents often come up to me at autism conferences and tell me that when their grandchildren were diagnosed, they realized they were autistic. In most cases, they had good jobs, in a roles such as a computer programmer, accountant, pharmacist, veterinarian, construction worker, or mechanic. These individuals were able to get and keep good jobs because they had learned working skills. They had paper routes in high school and worked summer jobs. However, I want to emphasize that it is never too late to start. The first step is for the individual to perform a task that is on a schedule where somebody outside the family is the boss. I recently met an autistic teenager who proudly told me that she was the "coffee lady" at her church. This is an example of a first step toward employment that can be easily set up in the community. There is no cost. Some other examples would be assisting an elderly person, or walking the neighbor's dog. It should be a neighbor's dog, so that the boss is outside the family. This will require being on time and following the neighbor's instructions. Many times, parents have told me that their autistic child "bloomed," "blossomed," and "came out of their shell" when they got a job they loved.

For me, having an interesting career has provided me with both friends and a life that has purpose. I had to learn sufficient social skills to keep my job. Social chit-chat for the sake of being social is boring. I love to talk about my favorite subjects with friends who have the same shared interest. One thing I had to learn was not to overdo it.

Some of the topics in this book that will be covered are the importance of learning a few basic social skills and having good hygiene. Being eccentric is fine, but you cannot be a rude, dirty slob. I chose to dress in a distinctive western style, and another autistic individual may choose to have colored hair. Expressing yourself with your own look is fine, but it must not be messy. Doing these basics helped me to get into a great career. There is also a section on both conventional medications and alternative treatments. Both of these have been helpful for me. Other sections cover getting and keeping jobs, finding mentors, getting workplace accommodations, and learning to drive. Throughout this book, I have used the term autistic instead of person with autism. Most people on the autism spectrum do this. Being autistic is part of who I am.

CHAPTER ONE

SOCIAL
FUNCTIONING

The way I see it, a huge mistake many teachers and parents make is to try to make autistic people into something they are not— turn the geeky nerd into an un-geek. I will never be a highly social un-geek.

THE SOCIAL BRAIN VERSUS THE AUTISTIC BRAIN

For me, the most interesting things in the world are animals, aerospace, and building things. The people I have the most fun socializing with are the ones who have similar interests. I love to geek out and discuss animal behavior, concrete-forming systems, or how to improve animal welfare. Many other people do not share my intense interest in these subjects, so I have learned that I can still be myself, but I limit the time I spend discussing them with people who have other interests. My best friends are those with whom I have shared special interests.

There are hundreds of papers in scientific literature about problems people on the autism spectrum have with social thinking and theory of mind (ToM). Theory of mind is the ability to understand what other people may be thinking. In its most elementary form, it's the ability to understand that different people have different thoughts. Involved with ToM is perspective taking, being able to think about and understand an event or a situation "through the eyes of another." These are all social thinking skills that develop without formal instruction in neurotypical individuals, starting at a very early age. These are also skills that most people, including educators, assume exist in all people, to a greater or lesser degree of development. This is not the case with autistic people. Everything has to be learned.

Uta Frith's theory of mind is similar to *context blindness*, described by Peter Vermeulen. A simple example of not understanding how other people would feel would be laughing at a funeral. Another example would be complaining about the food when you were invited to a charity banquet. That would hurt the host's feelings. However, there is another context where telling others that the breaded chicken was terrible would be appropriate. If I was working with the hotel banquet manager and the banquet planning committee, it would be appropriate to voice my opinion about not serving the breaded chicken meal. Autistic young adults who get out in the world and experience many different events can be mentored on the appropriate way to act. If they put lots of specific examples into their database, they will know how to act at similar events. A good mentor will explain why laughing at a funeral is not appropriate because the other people attending the funeral are sad.

Without a fully functioning social thinking system, autistic individuals who are fully verbal stumble along through academic and social situations, missing valuable bits of verbal nuance or nonverbal body messages that are woven into typical conversation. The impairment can be pervasive, even among those with higher intelligence. For instance, a middle school child who can wax eloquent about the anatomical differences among different varieties of alligators may not understand the simple social convention of turning his body toward his conversational partner to indicate interest in what he has to say. The alligator expert also needs to learn that not everybody wants to discuss alligators for over an hour. Neither verbal ability nor IQ is an indication of equivalent social aptitude and social thinking/reasoning skills. The most basic of social skills may be missing. In a highly intelligent person, social skills that come naturally to most people have to be learned. It is like learning how to act in a play.

I have always been able to pass a simple theory of mind test. An example of such a test would go like this. I am in a room with Jim and Bob. Bob puts a candy-bar in a box, and Jim leaves the room. While Jim is out of the room, Bob moves the candy bar from the box to a desk drawer. When Jim returns, I know that he thinks the candy bar is still in the box. If I had impaired theory of mind, I would think that Jim also knows the candy bar was moved to the desk drawer, because I saw him move the candy bar, and if I know it, so does everyone else.

I process this test purely with my photo-realistic visual thinking. I picture Jim outside with the door closed; he could not possibly see the candy bar being moved. When I was given a more complex theory of mind test, I did poorly because it required remembering a sequence of several events involving children and an ice cream truck. Plus, the test was presented verbally, which made remembering it even more difficult for my visual-thinking mind. My ability to remember spoken word sequence is absolutely terrible. When I ask for driving directions, I have to write them down to remember the sequence. With the second ToM test, my problem was not in understanding another person's viewpoint; it was with my sequencing skills. Written instructions in a checklist format are best for me, as they are for a majority of individuals with autism.

Visual Theory of Mind

My mother taught me when I was very young—again, by using visual examples—the importance of understanding how another person feels. When I was about eight, I ate with my mouth open, and Mother kept telling me to keep it closed when I was chewing my food. She kept telling me to close my mouth, but I still chewed with it open because it made no sense to me why it was important. Then one day I came home from school, and I told mother that watching Billy eat with his mouth open made me gag, that it looked like the inside of a garbage truck. Mother quietly replied, "Your mouth looks like the inside of a garbage truck when it is open, and it makes me want to gag." Now I understood that mother was experiencing the same response that I had experienced when I saw Billy chew with his mouth open. To understand how another person felt in the situation, I had to experience myself what the other child was experiencing. For children who are less visual learners and respond well to verbal language, it may work to tell them that the rule is to chew with their mouth closed.

Avoid Being Abstract

Conversely, it is also difficult for people who think in verbal abstractions to understand situations where nonverbal thinking may be an advantage. This can present career opportunities for people with autism. In my job designing livestock facilities, nothing is abstract. Verbal thinking is not required to design and build things, because I visualize them in my imagination. This is why I like my career so much. I get a great sense of accomplishment from improving conditions for animals, and now half the cattle in the US and Canada are handled in equipment I designed. I can see the tangible results of my work; it is not an abstract idea. I also get great satisfaction when I can help a parent or teacher solve a problem with a child. When parents tell me that one of my books helped them understand their child and enabled them to work with them more effectively, it makes me really happy.

To be an effective teacher for a child with autism, you must explain to them the rules of living in a nonabstract manner. Do not say to a child, "Well, you have to be good because it is the right thing to do." The words *good* and *right* are much too abstract for the concrete-thinking mind of the spectrum child. Instead, be specific and say, "You should take turns playing the game because, if another child was playing, you would want him to give you a turn to play." Another concrete example would be something like, "Do not steal the other child's toys, because you would not like it if he took your things." Teach the Golden Rule, one specific example at a time. In plain language, the

Golden Rule says, "Treat others the way you want to be treated." Concepts such as good or bad are learned with specific examples put into categories. There can also be degrees of good and bad that are learned with specific examples. For example, robbing a bank is worse than stealing an apple. Murder is worse than robbing a bank.

I Am What I Do

Another reason having a good career is so important to me is that I am what I do instead of what I feel. For me, emotional complexity is replaced with intellectual complexity. My greatest satisfaction in life comes from doing things. My best social interactions always involve activities with others with whom I share a common interest, such as building things or animal behavior. Many of my friends either work in animal behavior, are involved with building projects, or work on the animal welfare issue. I also have lots of good friends in the autism community. My career gives my life meaning. This is the way many "techies" feel. To me, intellectual reason and knowledge are extremely valuable. This is why I was so upset twenty years ago when the library at our university was flooded. I was upset about books and knowledge being destroyed.

Over the several decades I have been involved with the autism community, I have learned that some individuals on the spectrum share my way of relating to life and the world, and others do not. There are individuals with autism who have a few more social-emotional circuits connected in their brain, and for them, feelings and emotional connection with others are a bigger part of their functioning. This also, however, produces a greater level of frustration in many parts of their lives, such as friendships and dating. The life of celibacy that I lead would not be right for them. This spectrum of emotional differences in individuals with autism became even more illuminated for me while working with Sean Barron on our 2005 book, *Unwritten Rules of Social Relationships.* It was a real eye-opener for me to learn that two successful adults with autism can relate to the world so differently and see where we are almost the same in many ways, and where we are so different. Sean had a girlfriend and a good romantic relationship in his life; that is not a choice that would work for me. Romantic relationships based on emotions are not for me. I have seen too many autistic women get into abusive relationships.

Sensory-Based Empathy

I can empathize through my senses rather than in a more emotional manner. When I see cattle in the mud, I can empathize with how cold and miserable they feel. One of the things I can empathize with is physical hardship. When the home mortgage mess in 2007 caused many people to lose their homes, it made me angry. The shoeshine lady at the Denver airport lost her home after she took out an adjustable-rate mortgage that she did not understand and was unable to meet the escalated payments. When businesses take advantage of the poor and less educated of our society, it makes me mad. I did not ask where she was living, but I visualized that maybe she was living in the tunnels under the airport. That would be really miserable.

People on the spectrum often have a strong sense of social justice. This sense is probably on a separate brain current from the circuits that are responsible for emotional relatedness between people. This sense of social justice is within me, too. Every time I read another article about people losing their homes due to unethical business practices, it makes me furious.

When I took psychology classes in college, I studied Maslow's pyramid of needs. At the bottom are food, shelter, and safety, and at the top are the abstract ideals of self-actualization, a concept that remains nebulous to me.

I am much more concerned about the bottom of the pyramid. These things affect people's lives on a basic level. I want actual results, such as improving the handling of livestock or providing advice that helps an autistic adult get a job they really like. The only theory that interests me is that which results in real, tangible improvements happening on the ground level. In the autism world, that would be a theory that produces a good outcome for a child. A nonverbal child should have the opportunities to grow up and have a meaningful life in supportive living and possibly hold a job, depending on their level of functioning. There are some nonspeaking autistic people who can type independently and have normal or superior intelligence. To learn more, I recommend books written by nonspeaking autistic individuals such as Tito Mukhopadhyah and Naoki Higashida. People on the fully verbal end of the spectrum should be able to live independently, work, and contribute to society as their own interests and viewpoints dictate. For the really smart autistic individuals, a college education and a career is a reasonable goal. In my work with equipment design, I worked with metal fabrication shops that were owned by autistic people. They were brilliant and had many patents.

Some of the autistic individuals who feel emotional connectedness, who pursue not just social but romantic relationships, may find success in dating or marrying another person who shares their interests. Socialization through a shared interest, such as a science fiction or history club, are often where the first dates occur. I have talked to many neurotypical spouses who do not understand a husband who is autistic. They are concerned about his lack of social-emotional relatedness. The brain circuits may not be hooked up for emotional relatedness, but he can be a good provider, a good parent, and very loyal. These individuals often possess many good traits, such as honesty, dedication, steadfastness, and a sense of social justice, that can be good in a marriage. In my book Different Not Less, eighteen people write about their own experiences with getting diagnosed later in life. For many, it was a relief because it helped with personal relationships.

I Am a Nerd

The way I see it, a huge mistake many teachers and parents make is to try to make people with autism into something they are not—turn the geeky nerd into an un-geek, for instance. That just won't work. Teaching them to be socially functional is a worthy goal and one not to be overlooked. However, it would be in everybody's best interest to remember that the world is made up of all sorts of individuals, and that geeks, nerds, and people with fully verbal autism are often one and the same thing. I can learn social rules, but I will never have the undercurrent of social-emotional relatedness that exists in some people. The neural circuits that connect those parts of the brain just aren't hard-wired in me.

I have heard sad stories where a mother took her teenager out of computer classes that he truly enjoyed and placed him in situations to make him more social. That was a totally wrong thing to do for two reasons. First, it robbed him of the opportunity to develop a talent and interest that could lead to future employment. Second, the teen's social experiences would more naturally unfold and progress with the other computer students—those with whom he has shared interests. Robotics clubs, working with animals, art, and theater also provide great opportunities to make friends. The happy geeks excel at their jobs and get to work in Silicon Valley, where they are appreciated for their brains. The unhappy geeks end up without activities to keep them intellectually stimulated and, instead, are forced into uncomfortable social situations that, more often than not, fail to achieve the goal of making them more social. The people in the world who think that social connectedness is the ultimate goal of life forget that telephones, social networking websites, text messaging, and all the other electronic vehicles that fuel their passion for socializing are made by people with some degree of autism. Geeks swoon over the new technology they create; social addicts swoon by communicating with the technology and showing it off as a status symbol. Is one "better" than the other? I think not. A big problem for some autistic adults is excessive video game use. An hour or two a day is OK, but ten hours a day is an addiction. I have talked to five or six former video gamers who were introduced to car mechanics. They discovered that motors were more interesting than video games, and they are now employed as mechanics. Video games were gradually replaced with more and more hours of mechanics. Two young adults who are now mechanics told me that motors are more interesting than video games.

The Autistic Brain Is More Interested in Things

Dr. Nancy Minshew, University of Pittsburgh, did a functional MRI brain scan on me that indicated that I was innately more interested in looking at videos of things than videos of people. When I did the scan, I had no idea of its purpose. A series of short video clips of people and things, such as bridges, buildings, and fruit, were shown. I immediately noticed that the videos were old and scratchy and looked like they came from the 1970s. This triggered my mind into problem-solving mode to figure out where the researchers had gotten these old videos. The pictures of things provided more clues to the origin of the videos than the pictures of people. When the things flashed on the screen, I looked for cars because I wanted to know how old the videos were. My brain reacted by giving more neural activity to pictures of things than people.

There is no right or wrong in the interests and ways of being among individuals with autism, provided they can function reasonably well within society. If they cannot, further social learning is clearly needed.

When all else is relatively equal, the way I see it, parents and educators should respect the innate interests of the child and nurture their expression. To develop interests that could develop into a career, autistic kids need to be exposed to many different things, such as art, Legos, and musical instruments. A big problem I see is parents and teachers often fail to broaden a fixed narrow interest. It is a shame when the Lego builder may never graduate to using tools. My mother broadened my drawing skills from drawing single horse heads to drawing things related to horses. A teenager's interest in a single type of car could be broadened by joining a car club, doing math involving the favorite car, and learning how the engine works.

Not everyone in the world is highly social, and that's a good thing. It's the same within the autism spectrum. In another case I learned about, a boy with more severe autism was a great artist. His mother was so upset that he would never marry (her dream for her son), she was hesitant to help him develop his artistic ability. For this kid, art was his life. Fortunately, she was persuaded to start a business selling her son's art. He is content to draw all day, and this gives his life meaning.

The autism spectrum is broad. Many individuals are blessed with a unique ability, while others do not have any special skills. But each individual, no matter what level of skills or social abilities, can become a contributing member of the community. This is what will give meaning to their lives. Our goal, therefore, is not to make these individuals find meaning in our lives, but for us to help individuals with autism find meaning in their own lives.

Additional Reading

Coutelle, R. et al. (2021) Autism Spectrum Disorder and video games: Restricted interest or addition? *International Journal of Mental Health and Addictions*, March 8, 2021.

Grandin, T. (2019) How horses helped a teenager with autism make friends and learn how to work, *Int. J. Environ. Res. Public Health*, 2019, July 1;16(13):2325, doi:10.3390/ijerph16132325.

Grandin, T. (2024) *Grandin Papers*, Future Horizons, Arlington, Texas.

Grandin, T. (2001) Transferring results of behavioral research to industry to improve animal welfare on the farm, ranch, and slaughter plant. *Applied Animal Behavior Science*.

Higashida, Naoki (2017) *Fall Down 7 Times, Get Up 8*, Random House, New York.

Mukhopadhyah, Tito Rajarshi (2008) *How Can I Talk if My Lips Don't Move?* Arcade Publishing, New York.

Wikipedia (2024) "Maslow's Hierarchy of Needs."

Vermeulen, P. (2012) *Autism as Context Blindness*, Future Horizons, Arlington, Texas.

INSIGHTS INTO AUTISTIC
SOCIAL PROBLEMS

An interesting study by Dr. Ami Klin and associates at the Yale Child Study Center is helping to explain some of the social problems in people with autism. Both normal and autistic adults were fitted with a device that electronically tracked their eye movements, allowing the researchers to determine what the person was looking at. Subjects wearing the eye-tracking device were shown digitized clips of *Who's Afraid of Virginia Woolf?*, a movie that contains a high number of instances of social interaction between people in a living room setting. (It is the kind of movie I find boring because of its social nature.)

The first finding was that autistic subjects fixated on the mouths of people instead of on their eyes. I think one of the reasons they do this is because of their problems hearing auditory detail. I have problems hearing hard consonant sounds. If somebody says "brook," I know the word is not "crook" if it is spoken in the context of a picnic. Looking at the mouth of the person talking makes hearing the correct word easier. I find that when I am in a noisy room, hearing is more difficult if I look at a person's eyes. I tend to point my good ear toward the person, in order to hear better.

Amy Klin's study also showed that a normal person's gaze rapidly switched back and forth between the eyes of the two people conversing in the movie. This happened with less frequency in a person with autism. In one particular test, the subjects viewed three people conversing. The autistic person's gaze switched only once, while the normal subject's gaze moved at least six times among the three people on the screen. This can be explained by attention-shifting delays and the slow brain processing speed that is often present in autism. Research conducted by Eric Courchesne in San Diego has shown that autistics take much longer to shift attention between two different stimuli than their normal counterparts. The inability to shift attention quickly may explain some of the social deficits that develop within this population. Even if a person with autism was more aware of social cues that go on between people, their inability to quickly shift focus would prevent them from catching these short, silent messages that people frequently use to communicate nonverbally.

Problems Caused by Slow Brain Processing Speed:

- Difficulty with rapid multi-tasking jobs
- Slow to respond when asked a question
- Rapid back-and-forth conversation is difficult
- Poor working memory for sequential instructions presented verbally (recommend written checklists)
- Auditory processing problems, such as not hearing hard consonant sounds
- Interrupting conversation because the pauses in the conversation go by too quickly.

Processing the meaning of eye movements requires many rapid attention shifts. This may partially explain why people with autism may not even be aware of subtle eye movements that often occur during conversations. I did not know that people communicated with their eye movements until I read about it in a book in my early fifties. All my life I existed unaware of this part of communication. As a child, I understood that if a person's head was pointed toward me, they could see me. But I did not notice smaller eye movements. Many adults with autism have commented that they finally discovered at a later age that normal people have a language in their eyes; however, they could never understand it. Not being able to rapidly shift attention may be the reason why.

I went back and re-read the Ami Klin paper. There was another clip from the same movie where the autistic gaze was quicker. It was a situation which could be dangerous. One of the characters went to the closet and unwrapped a gun. I also react quickly to danger. When a candleholder on the wall started a fire that flared up the wood panels, I jumped up and threw water on it. Mother thought I overreacted. It is likely I may have saved our house. The brain also has a quick low road circuit. It enables both people and animals to make almost reflexive responses to avoid danger. The circuit bypasses all the higher brain functions. Joseph LeDoux, a neuroscientist, called it the "low road" and "high road' brain circuits.

Masking Can Be Exhausting

Devon Price, in her book *Unmasking Autism,* explains that autistic people will compensate and act more "normal" by masking. They may "camouflage" to obscure autistic traits or compensate to appear nondisabled. Continuous masking and covering up autistic behaviors can be exhausting and may lead to depression or anxiety. Samuel Arnold and colleagues in Australia studied autistic burnout. This may occur when masking becomes too exhausting. One lady on the spectrum told me that if she was exhausted at the end of the day, she had done too much masking. I have difficulty following rapid-paced back-and-forth conversation. My brain's slow processing speed cannot keep up. Following stand-up comedians who talk fast is extremely difficult.

My approach to masking is a small amount of it is necessary, but I will never be the purely social person. I have learned to be polite and not bore people with endless conversations about my favorite subjects. Fortunately, I have some friends who like to geek out and discuss the same favorite subject.

Avoiding masking must never be used as an excuse for really rude behavior. Some examples would be pushing and shoving in line at the grocery store or walking up to strangers and calling them swear words. I actually had an autistic man do this to me at an autism meeting. All this does is close channels of communication and alienate them from others. There are some social "niceties" that you should always do, such as saying "please" and "thank you." They require very little effort.

Additional Reading

Arnold, S. et al. (2023) Confirming the nature of autistic burnout. *Autism* (In Press).

Andeou, M. et al. (2020) Theory of mind deficits and neurophysiological operatives in autism spectrum disorders: A Review *Brain Sciences* 10(6), 393.

Cremen, I.M. et al. (2023) Measuring social camouflaging in individuals with high functioning autism: A literature review, *Brain Sciences*, 13, 469.

Hill, E.L. and Frith, U. (2003) Understanding autism: Insights from mind and brain, Philosophical Transactions of the Royal Society of London, *Biological Sciences*, 358(1430):281-289.

Klin, A. et al. (2002) Defining and quantifying the social phenotype in autism. *American Journal of Psychiatry*, 159:895-908.

Klin, A. et al. (2002) Visual fixation patterns during viewing of naturalistic social situations as predictors of social competence in individuals with autism, *Archives of General Psychiatry*, 59(9):809-816.

The anger and resentment many people with autism feel is understandable and justified. What is not, however, is rude "acting-out behavior" in response to these feelings.

A FEW BASIC SOCIAL SKILLS ARE ESSENTIAL

I went to a large autism meeting here in the US and was appalled at the rude behavior exhibited by a few adult autistic individuals who were also attending. One of them walked up to me and said, "Who the (swear word) are you?" He also interrupted two major sessions at the conference because he adamantly opposed the speaker's opinions. Later that day, this same individual ran a panel discussion where individuals with AS talked about their lives. During this session, his manners and behavior were polite and perfect, demonstrating he was capable of behaving properly when he wanted to.

What was most distressing to me was that these individuals felt that because they had autism, the people around them should accept their rude behavior—that their "disability" made them somehow exempt from all social standards we all live by. Like it or not, social boundaries exist, and we are expected to learn a few basic social skills.

I agreed with some of the viewpoints of these autistic individuals, but they could have been much more effective in the delivery of their message by not being rude. Then other people at the conference would have been willing to listen to them and consider what they had to say. Rude behavior has consequences, and in most cases, they are negative. In general, rude or overt antisocial behavior does the following:

- Turns people off instantly. Most people dislike those who are rude.
- Makes people uncomfortable, uneasy.
- Closes down channels of communication.
- Results in people forming quick negative opinions about you, whether or not they are valid or based on fact.
- Alienates you from others, reducing the chance of further contact.
- Makes a person look weak, like they are unable to be in control of their emotions.

Those of us with autism live in a society that can be grossly ignorant of our needs, of the day-by-day difficulty we face in trying to "fit" into a world that is often harsh, stressful, and grating on our neurology. The anger and resentment many people with autism feel are understandable and justified. What is not, however, is rude "acting-out behavior" in response to these feelings and calling that behavior acceptable in the name of autism.

The autism and neurotypical cultures remain divided, yet that gap is slowly closing through education, awareness, and experiences. It happens one person at a time, and we each play a role in how quickly we close the gap. When individuals with autism tout a rigid belief that they should be allowed to act in any way they choose, exempt from all social rules that call for respect for our fellow human beings, they widen the chasm that still exists. It perpetuates a we-versus-them mentality: "You are wrong; we are right." It also perpetuates the very negative stereotypes some of us on the spectrum work to overturn: that people with AS are stubborn, resistant to change, and unwilling to compromise. While these may be characteristics of autism, to put forth the notion that these are immutable, unchangeable personality traits only further supports the "inability" of people on the spectrum.

The best way to teach the child is to use "teachable" moments. When a child makes a social mistake, do not scream, "NO." Instead, give instruction. For example, if a child reaches across the dining room table for the food, tell him to ask his mother or sister to pass it.

If a child pushes in line at the movie theater, tell him, "You have to wait your turn for a ticket." If he makes a rude comment about a person at the grocery store, pull him aside and say, "It is rude to discuss other people's appearance in public." The key is to calmly give instruction and not start screaming at the child.

The teachable moment also works with adults. On my first project, I criticized some welding and said it looked like pigeon doo doo. The plant engineer was a great job coach. In private, he calmly told me what I should do, and he made me apologize for the rude talk. To get along in the world, an autistic person should conform to some basic social rules. On the other hand, I would become exhausted if I always tried to not interrupt and follow very rapid conversations. My processing speed is too slow to find the natural break in the conversation. There is a need for some compromise.

Gentle Pushing and Providing Choices

My mother knew just how hard to push to get me to tackle new challenges. She always gave me some choices. She never forced me into a new situation I could not handle. When I was afraid to visit my aunt's ranch, she gave me a choice. I could stay for a week or stay all summer. I got to the ranch and loved it. I see too many parents who won't let go and instead do everything for their child. There are many fully verbal teenagers who have never gone shopping by themselves. Christine Romeo, the mother of Abby Romeo, told the audience at a recent disability conference, "You have to pull back to let your child have some growth." Her autistic daughter now has many successes, such as being on the award-winning show *Love on the Spectrum* and in popular music videos. Both my mother and Christine believe in the importance of developing strengths.

I have talked to many parents who have told me their child is good at drawing or some other skill but keeps destroying their work because it has some minor imperfection.

THE NEED TO BE PERFECT

Some individuals on the autism spectrum who are good at drawing or other skills will often destroy excellent work because it is not absolutely perfect. Sean Barron, a well-known individual on the spectrum, described how he destroyed a beautiful airplane he had made—one that had taken many, many hours to create— because it had one small flaw. In his mind, if the plane was not perfect, it had no value. Other individuals will delete good artwork from their computer because they think it is inferior. Some children will tear up pages of homework because of one small spelling correction or because too much erasing makes the page look messy.

Other individuals on the autism spectrum conceal their ability. One mother discovered that her nonverbal son, who, to her knowledge, could not read, was typing words such as "depression" into Google. This is very different than a child or adult typing a memorized cartoon character's name into YouTube so he can watch videos. Memorizing a cartoon character's name requires no reading skills, but typing words such as "depression" or "Iraq" may indicate an individual has some hidden reading skills. I told his mother to download the computer's cache memory to look at her son's search history to determine if he was possibly reading about "Iraq" or was just exposed to the word by the people around him. By looking at his search history, the mother could determine if her son might be concealing his reading ability.

Even Experts Are Not Perfect

People with autism tend toward black-and-white thinking. They see themselves and the world around them in polar opposites, and this tendency feeds their need to be perfect. Even the tiniest mistakes and mishaps can feel like monumental failures to them, creating high levels of anxiety when their efforts or the events around them do not measure up to this all-or-nothing scale.

I have talked to many parents who have told me their child is good at drawing or some other skill but keeps destroying their work because it has some minor imperfection. It is important for parents to teach a child, in concrete ways, that (1) skills exist on a continuum and (2) there are different levels of quality required for different levels of work. To start, explain to the child that even the greatest experts in a field may have imperfections in their work. For example, being a photographer for *National Geographic* requires a person to be the very best. A photographer for *The New York Times* has to be good, but not as good as a photographer for *National Geographic*. In other words, there are different levels of quality for photography work. They could be listed like this:

- Expert photographer—works at *National Geographic*
- Very good photographer—works at *New York Times* or *Wall Street Journal*
- Good photographer—works doing local weddings, portraits, or local commercial photography
- Good amateur—takes nice scenic vacation pictures
- Snapshot taker—takes snapshots of average quality
- Terrible photographer—takes totally bad pictures: cuts off heads, takes blurry pictures, or makes other immediately obvious mistakes

As the quality categories of the photos decline, the pictures will contain more and more mistakes. It is equally important that an individual sees concrete examples of the best and the worst to develop perspective. If you look hard enough, it is even possible to find mistakes in photos in *National Geographic* magazines; not all their photos are absolutely perfect. A person can have a good career in photography if his pictures are in categories 1, 2, or 3.

Giving individuals concrete visual representations of the different levels of photography can help them better understand the continuum of skills. A mentor or teacher can reinforce these ideas, showing the individual many examples of photos for each category and even helping the individual sort photos into the different categories. The individual can then strive for *National Geographic* or *Time Magazine* quality instead of perfection. When the student looks at one of his own photos, he can be reinforced to ask himself, "Is this good enough for categories 1, 2, or 3?" instead of getting angry and destroying his work because it is not perfect.

When I was getting started, I had the opposite problem. I sometimes did sloppy work on tasks that did not interest me. In my twenties, I did a very sloppy job making copies of sales brochures. A good way to instruct me would have been to show me an example of a quality copy job and contrast that with an example of a poor copy job while explaining what makes one good and the other bad. For instance, crooked copies are not acceptable. Copies missing any pages are not acceptable. The quality of work can be measured along a range from excellent (though not totally perfect) to terrible. These categories are similar to the thermometer scales used with individuals with autism to teach different levels of emotions.

A quality scale can be used in many different applications, from writing to computer programming. For writing, the categories could range from major literary works to local newspaper writing to poor school papers. Make sure students see specific examples of each category.

A Perfect World Does Not Exist

It took me a while to learn that even the best workplaces are not perfect. Recently, I talked to a young autistic employee who was having problems at work. She worked at a good workplace and had a good boss, but other employees were sometimes mean and broke the rules. I told her about a simple logical process to help make decisions about whether or not to keep her job, telling her to stay if the good things about the workplace outweighed the bad. I visualize weighing good and bad as an old-fashioned balance scale. Below is an example to show how to look at both good and bad things.

Examples of Possible Good Things:

- I can walk to work.
- I like my boss.
- I like helping customers.
- The business does not exploit people and rip them off.
- The pay is decent.

Examples of Possible Bad Things:

- There is one employee there that I dislike.
- An employee smokes in the breakroom.
- I do not agree with the owner's political views.

I would keep my job at this business, but there is a line I would not cross. Early in my career, I worked for a construction company and handled advertising. When I was told to place ads in cattle magazines that I knew they would not pay for, it was time to quit. I would not steal from the cattle magazine. I would work for an employer who had political views I did not agree with, but I would quit if asked to actively participate in the owner's political activities.

The autistic person must learn that perfection does not exist. There are degrees of goodness and badness. For example, smoking in the break room breaks a rule, but it is minor compared to stealing. Tattling to the manager will make other employees hate you, but I would not work for a company that had me participate in stealing.

LEARNING SOCIAL RULES

C hildren and adults on the autism spectrum are concrete, literal thinkers. Ideas that can't be understood through logic or that involve emotions and social relationships are difficult for us to grasp, and even more difficult to incorporate into our daily lives.

When I was in high school, figuring out the social rules was a major challenge. It was not easy to notice similarities in people's social actions and responses because they were often inconsistent from person to person and situation to situation. Over time, I observed that some rules could be broken with minor consequences, and other rules, when broken, had serious consequences. It perplexed me that other kids seemed to know which rules they could bend and break and which rules must never be broken. They had a flexibility of thinking that I did not have. I knew I had to learn these rules if I wanted to function in social situations. If I had to learn them, they somehow had to be meaningful to me, to make sense to me within my own way of thinking and viewing the world. I started observing others as would a scientist and discovered I could group the rules into an organizational format to which I could relate into major and minor categories. By the time I was a senior in high school, I had a system for categorizing some of the social rules of life. I still use the same system today.

I developed four rule categories:

1. Really Bad Things
2. Courtesy Rules
3. Illegal but Not Bad
4. Sins of the System

Really Bad Things

I reasoned that in order to maintain a civilized society, there must be prohibitions against doing really bad things, such as murder, arson, rape, stealing, looting, and injuring other people. If really bad things are not controlled, a civilized society where we have jobs, food in the stores, and electricity cannot exist.

The prohibition against really bad things is universal in all civilized societies. Children need to be taught that cheating—in all forms, not just on tests—is bad. Learning to "play fair" will help a child grow into an adult who will not commit really bad things. The child can be taught the concept of playing fair with many specific examples.

Courtesy Rules

All civilized societies have courtesy rules, such as saying "please" and "thank you." These rules are important because they help prevent anger that can escalate into really bad things. Different societies have different courtesy rules, but they all serve the same function. In most countries, some common courtesy rules are as follows: standing and waiting your turn in a line, having good table manners, being neat and clean, giving up your seat on a bus to an elderly person, or raising your hand and waiting for the teacher to point to you before speaking in class.

Illegal but Not Bad

These rules can sometimes be broken depending upon the circumstance. Rules in this category vary greatly from one society to another, and how an individual views these rules will be influenced by his or her own set of moral and personal beliefs. Be careful though. Consequences for breaking some are minor, but there may be a fine for others. Included in this category is slight speeding in cars. One rule I often recommend breaking is the age require-ment for attending a community college. I tell parents to sign up the child so he can escape being teased in high school. However, the parent must impress upon the child that this is a grown-up privilege and the child must obey all the courtesy rules. An example of a rule that would not fall in this category would be running a red light. Doing this carries the possibility of injuring or killing someone, which is a really bad thing.

Sins of the System

These are rules that must never be broken, although they may seem to have little or no basis in logic. Rules in this category often vary greatly between different countries and societies. They must simply be accepted within a par-ticular country or culture. For instance, a small sexual transgression that would result in your name being added to a sex offender list in the US may have little or no consequence in another country. In the US, we are allowed to criticize politicians or the government. In other countries, it may be a sin of the system and you could go to jail. In the US, the four major sins of the system are sexual transgressions, drug offenses, making fake IDs, and playing with explosives. Several parents have reported to me that their teenager looked at child porn and ended up on the sex offender list. It may be a good idea to show teenagers the sex offender website and explain to them that being listed as a sex offender will ruin your life and career. Autistic teens and adults must be taught that they NEVER, NEVER text or post photos of their private parts. First of all, they must be made aware of the laws. Forced sex (rape), sex with underage people, or looking at child porn has the penalty of prison and being placed on the sex offender list. The laws vary by state on the severity of the penalties. Adolescents need to know the rules and be very careful where they go online. If they play video games online with other people, they need to go to well-known, safe sites. If the conversation during a game goes off the topic of the game, they need to log off. Autistic teens and adults need to have relationships, but it may be best to do dates in person with people in their community.

In a post-September 11 world, pranks that used to be considered kids being naughty are now being prosecuted as serious crimes. Never commit a sin of the system because the penalties are usually very severe.

This method of categorizing social rules has worked well for me. However, each person with autism may need different rule categories that make sense for him or her. The number of sins of the system is increasing. NEVER make threats online or in person to harm or kill people. Threats are NEVER a joke. You can go to jail.

**My emotions are all in the present. I can be angry,
but I get over it quickly.**

EMOTIONAL DIFFERENCES AMONG INDIVIDUALS WITH AUTISM

I gained some valuable insight into both myself and others on the autism spectrum when I worked with Sean Barron on our book, *Unwritten Rules of Social Relationships: Decoding Social Mysteries Through the Unique Perspectives of Autism.* There were areas where Sean and I shared similar emotions and other areas where emotional relatedness was experienced almost opposite one another. We both are independent, well-functioning adults, with varied interests and social relationships, yet our social-emotional development took very different paths.

We were similar in two main areas: rigid, black-and-white thinking and singular obsessions. In elementary school, Sean obsessed over the exact angle of parked school buses. My obsession was collecting election and wrestling posters. Both of us bored other people silly talking about our favorite things.

We also shared a rigid thinking style. Sean describes how he built an airplane from Tinkertoys and became enraged when one small, inconsequential part had been left out. Instead of taking pride in his accomplishment and realizing how minor the little part was, he smashed the airplane to pieces. In his mind, you either built the model correctly, or you failed. I had a similar experience when I started designing cattle corrals. One of my early clients was not completely satisfied with my work. I did not realize it is impossible to please everybody. In my mind, his dissatisfaction meant I might have to give up cattle corral design forever. Fortunately, my good friend Jim Uhl, the contractor who built the corrals, talked me into continuing my design work.

Emotionally, Sean and I are very different. I solve social problems with logic and "instant replays" of the mistakes I made, using my strongly visual imagination. I analyze these photo-realistic replays of social missteps as a football coach would analyze his team's maneuvers. My satisfaction in life comes through interests I can share with other people and a challenging career. Sean is a word thinker; he has to figure things out in words and emotions. He feels connected to people via his emotions. Where I replaced emotional complexity with intellectual complexity, Sean strove to gain social-emotional relatedness.

My emotions are all in the present. I can be angry, but I get over it quickly. When I replay scenes, the emotions are no longer attached to them. Sean had a lingering, seething anger I do not have. More like so-called "normal" people, he can get angry, and it can simmer like a pot on a stove. In our book, Sean describes becoming jealous of his dog's social skills. It made him jealous that his parents and sister responded more positively to the dog than to him. It would have never crossed my mind to be jealous of a dog's social skills.

However, Sean picked up more social cues than I did. If people tolerated me and did not tease or yell, I was satisfied. When I first started visiting feedlots, the cowboys thought I was totally weird. As long as they allowed me to help work cattle, I was happy. Their impressions of me didn't cause me hardship or sad feelings. To fit into my work environment, I had to prove my worth by being really good at what I did. I sold my skills and work, not my personality. With Sean, the feeling of "being connected" was more important.

Unwritten Rules contains many examples of the social-emotional similarities and differences between Sean and me. However, the basic difference in how Sean and I perceive the world is this: I am what I do, and Sean's sense of being is what he feels. In the future, brain scans will be able to identify the differences between individuals' social-emotional functioning. I speculate that Sean, and individuals on the spectrum like him, have a few more social-emotional neural connections in their brain than do I, or individuals like me, with stronger visual, logical processing styles.

(*Unwritten Rules of Social Relationships: Decoding Social Mysteries Through the Unique Perspectives of Autism* by Temple Grandin, Sean Barron, and Veronica Zysk won a prestigious Silver Award in *Foreword Magazine*'s 2005 Book of the Year competition.)

European studies are showing that mindfulness training is helpful for both anxiety and depression. Many books and local classes are available. One study was done by Esther de Bruin in the Netherlands. Willem Kuyken at Oxford University, along with other physicians, conducted a successful randomized trial using mindfulness training for depression.

In the old days, the diagnosis was *gifted*, not *disabled*. Attitudes strongly influence how we perceive spectrum kids today.

HEALTHY SELF-ESTEEM

One of the most pivotal reasons I think I was able to succeed in the neurotypical world as an adult was because Mother fostered a strong, healthy sense of self-worth in me as a young child. It wasn't one particular thing she did that other parents didn't do. Actually, in the '50s and '60s, consciously building your child's self-esteem wasn't part of the psychology of parenting. Back then kids just naturally did more things together, especially outdoor activities, because there weren't video games, streaming services, and computers to capture solitary attention indoors like there is today.

Even so, I think Mother unconsciously realized two important things about self-esteem:

- Self-esteem is built little by little, through real achievements. For instance, when I created beautiful embroidery, that project took time, effort, and patience to complete and made me feel good about myself.
- The literal, concrete mind of the autistic child requires that self-esteem be built through tangible accomplishments, coupled with verbal praise.

The "fix it" mentality that seems more prevalent today wasn't part of my younger years either. While I did have speech therapy in elementary school and would visit a psychiatrist once a month, both of these activities were conducted in a manner that, to me, didn't feel like something was wrong with me that needed "fixing." Nowadays, kids are being whisked off to one evaluation after another and go from therapy program to therapy program, some five or more days a week. What message is that sending children other than that parts of them are somehow unacceptable, or that their autism is bad? I think the intellectually gifted child suffers the most. Autistic children with IQs of 140+ are being held back by too much "handicapped" psychology. I have told several parents of brilliant AS children that in the old days, the diagnosis was *gifted*, not *disabled*. Attitudes strongly influence how we perceive spectrum kids today.

Throughout elementary school, I felt pretty good about myself. I flourished with the many projects I created, the praise they received from family and teachers, the friendships I shared, and the new experiences I mastered. When I won a trophy at winter carnival, that made me happy. When Mother had me sing at an adult concert when I was in sixth grade, I felt good about that. Even during the difficult high school years, my special interests kept me moving forward. I could revert to my hobbies when things got tough socially. They helped me get through those years.

Today, kids are being reinforced for the littlest things. It's setting up a cycle of needing approval for every little thing they do. *The Wall Street Journal* has run many articles lately about young kids entering the workforce who need constant praise from their manager or they can't get their job done. Parents and teachers need to take a look at how they're reinforcing children. As a child ages, the amount of praise they receive from others falls off dramatically. A child who constantly receives praise for making efforts in the social arena will face a rude awakening later in life, which can negatively affect his motivation to stay socially involved. It's a catch-22, and one that needs more attention than it's currently being given.

I wasn't praised all the time by Mother or my teachers; far from it. Neither were other kids. We were praised when we did something significant, so the praise was really meaningful and was a strong motivator. The everyday things, such as behaving at dinner, in church, or when we visited Aunt Bella, were not praised. It was just expected that I would behave. But when I made a beautiful clay horse in third grade, Mother really praised that.

Parents can start kids on the road to healthy self-esteem by offering praise associated with something concrete they can see or touch or smell. This has real meaning to the literal, concrete thinking mind of the autistic child. Especially when kids are young, encouraging them to engage in activities with visible, tangible outcomes helps them learn the direct connection between their actions and their abilities, their sense of mastery and control over their world. You can't build things or paint pictures or create anything concrete without making choices, learning sequencing skills, seeing how parts relate to a whole, and learning concepts and categories. This, in turn, lays the groundwork for more advanced skills to form, skills indigenous to the less-concrete world of social interactions.

Try building self-esteem in your child from the outside in, starting with tangible projects, and your child will find his own self-esteem blossoming from the inside out.

For me, social thinking skills largely developed over time and through repeated experiences.

FOUR CORNERSTONES OF SOCIAL AWARENESS

Achieving social success is dependent upon certain core attributes of the person with autism. In our book *Unwritten Rules of Social Relationships*, my co-author, Sean Barron, and I introduce four aspects of thinking and functioning we think contribute the most to successful social awareness and social interactions. These Four Cornerstones of Social Awareness are as follows:

- *Perspective taking:* the ability to put ourselves in another person's shoes—to understand that people can have similar or different viewpoints, emotions, and responses from our own. At an even more basic level is acknowledging that people exist and that they are sources of information to help us make sense of the world.

- *Flexible thinking:* the ability to accept change and be responsive to changing conditions and the environment; the mental ability to notice and process alternatives in both thought and actions; the ability to compare, contrast, evaluate.

- *Positive self-esteem:* a "can-do" attitude that develops through experiencing prior success and forms the basis for risk-taking in the child or adult. Self-esteem is built upon repeated achievements that start small and are concrete and become less tangible and more complex.

- *Motivation:* a sustained interest in exploring the world and working toward internal and external goals, despite setbacks and delays.

Often, motivation needs to be encouraged in kids with autism, especially within the social arena. Let the child feel the benefits of motivation first through using the child's favorite topics or special interests, and then slowly broadening out into other activities. If the child loves trains, teach reading, math, and writing with train-centered books, examples, and activities. Play train-themed games to motivate social interaction.

Based on the social understanding Sean and I have achieved in our lives, we emphatically agree that perspective taking, being able to look beyond one-self and into the mind of another person, is the *single most important aspect of functioning that determines the level of social success* to be achieved by a child or adult with autism. Through it we learn that what we do affects others—in positive and negative ways. It's the link that allows us to feel connected to others. It gives us the ability to consider our own thoughts in relation to the information we process about a social situation and then develop a response that contributes to, rather than detracts from, the social experience.

In our book, Sean describes how "talk therapy," as he called it, helped him develop better social thinking skills and appreciate the varied perspectives of other people in his life. During his middle and high school years, he and his parents would sit for hours, sometimes until 1:00 or 2:00 AM, discussing the most basic concepts of how relationships worked. For instance, Sean explains that even in his late teens, he still didn't understand why it wasn't okay to "absorb" people who took a genuine interest in him and showed they cared about him—that is, why it wasn't acceptable to spend all the time he wanted with someone who was much older and had family and other personal obligations. He couldn't understand why they wouldn't make him the centerpiece of their lives as did his parents.

For me, social thinking skills largely developed over time and through repeated experiences. The more social data I put on my mental hard drive, the better able I was to see the connections between my own thoughts and actions and those of others. For me, these social equations were born from my logical mind: "If I do X, then the majority of people will respond with Y." As I acquired more and more data through direct experience, I formed categories and subcategories and even more refined subcategories in my social thinking. That's why it's so important for parents to engage children in all sorts of different activities and experiences. Without that direct learning—and lots of it—children don't have the information they need to make these social connections in their thinking.

Perspective taking works hand in hand with flexible thinking; it provides opportunities for experiencing success in social interactions, which in turn fosters positive self-esteem. It can also act as a source of internal motivation, especially as children grow into adults and the type and quality of social interaction expands.

Social thinking skills must be directly taught to children and adults with autism. Parents, teachers, and service providers are slowly starting to realize the importance of incorporating such lessons into the child's overall education plan. Doing so opens doors of social understanding in all areas of life.

CHAPTER TWO

MEDICATIONS & BIOMEDICAL ISSUES

Kids are often put on way too many medications. If a medication or supplement is given, you should try one thing at a time to determine if it works.

A utism has captured attention within mainstream medicine (pharmaceutical companies) and within the realm of complementary and alternative medicine. One might assume this is good news, and to a degree, it is. As we learn more about the spectrum of autism and the individuals within it, valid, effective treatment options have been developed. However, not all companies have the best interests of individuals with autism and their families at the heart of their business. Profit motives run deep, and snake oil salesmen never go away. New interventions with slick public relations and marketing campaigns attached to them lure susceptible parents with promises of overnight success and, in some cases, a cure for autism. While some interventions are touted as based on research, closer inspection may reveal that "research" was done on a handful of individuals, sometimes carefully selected so that the intended results are achieved. Not all research is good research. Now more than ever, parents and caregivers need to be educated consumers of autism treatments and carefully evaluate all treatment options, especially those that sound too good to be true.

The articles in this section will help guide you in making good medication and biomedical decisions. You must think logically about the use of both conventional medications and alternative biomedical treatments such as special diets. The content on this section is not intended to be a substitute for individual professional medical advice, diagnosis or treatment. In 2006, I completely updated the medical section in my popular book, *Thinking in Pictures*. Rather than repeat information here, I'd like to relate some of my personal experiences with medication and biomedical interventions, along with an update on new research since 2006.

In this section, there will be no great new medication discoveries. Most of the new drugs are slight modifications of old generic drugs. They have no advantages and are much more expensive.

I am one of the many people in the autism community who was saved by antidepressant medication. Throughout my twenties, I had problems with constant anxiety and panic attacks that got worse and worse. I would wake up in the middle of the night with my heart pounding. Going to a new place sometimes brought on waves of panic, and I would almost choke when eating. If I had not started antidepressant medication in my early thirties, I would have been incapacitated by constant anxiety and stress-related colitis, which was wrecking my health. My professional life—the part of my world that brings me so much happiness—would have suffered tremendously.

After consultation and discussion about medication options with my doctor, I started taking Tofranil (imipramine) in 1980. Within a week, the anxiety and panic was 90 percent gone. No drug can provide 100 percent control of symptoms, and I avoided the temptation to take more of the drug every time I had a minor anxiety episode. Three years later, I switched to Norpramin (desipramine), and it has worked consistently well at the same low starter dose for over forty years. Another benefit was that my stress-related health problems stopped. Colitis attacks and pounding headaches ceased. Today, one of the second-generation SSRI (selective serotonin reuptake inhibitor) antidepressants such as Prozac (fluoxetine), Zoloft (sertraline), or Lexapro (Escitalopram) would be a better choice. (The use of the newer types of antidepressants is discussed in one of the sections in this chapter.) Since my old drug still works, I am not going to risk switching it.

To keep my medication working, I also turned my attention to supplemental therapies that improve physical functioning. I started incorporating lots of exercise into my daily regime. I do one hundred sit-ups every night.

Numerous scientific studies clearly show the benefits of exercise on the brain. Physical exercise can also help reduce anxiety, a common problem among spectrum children and adults. Living in Colorado and traveling as extensively as I do, light therapy during the winter months is also helpful. The Mayo Clinic has a helpful website titled Seasonal Affective Disorders: Choosing a Light Box. It really helps prevent the dark winter "blues." During the months of November, December, January, and February, I get up at 6:00 in the morning, while it's still dark, and use the light therapy for at least thirty minutes. This extends my photoperiod to be more like summer, which in turn has increased my energy during winter. I feel so much better. If I have trouble sleeping, one or two magnesium pills calm me down. It is not a megadose. Each 250 mg pill provides 67 percent of the daily requirement.

Can I ever stop taking my medication? Countless people cause tremendous problems for themselves when they relapse after quitting an effective medication that controlled their condition. Sometimes a previously effective medication fails to work when it is restarted. The person can end up in a worse position than before the medication was started. At present, there is a lack of research on long-term management of depression, bipolar disorder, and many other conditions. Funding from pharmaceutical companies mainly pays for short-term studies on medication usage. There is no research to tell me if I can safely stop taking desipramine now that I am 76. Since my condition is stable, I do not want to take the risk of experimenting when there is no research to guide me. I am on a single drug, and it works. I plan to keep taking it.

I want to emphasize that the autism spectrum is very variable. Some people with autism never experience severe enough anxiety, panic, or depression to warrant medication. Their physical nature, their body chemistry, is such that they can remain calm and level functioning. There are others who need some medication to get through puberty and then they can stop taking it. People with minor depression can often wean themselves off medication, especially if they are getting counseling or cognitive therapy in tandem with their drug use. But people with severe depression, constant panic attacks, and bipolar disorder, and people like me—whose body chemistry is out of kilter—are likely to experience major setbacks if they suddenly stop taking medication.

Avoid Medication Problems

A frequent mistake often made with medication use is increasing the dose or adding new medications every time the individual has an aggressive or anxious episode. I repeat an earlier bit of advice: the use of medications is serious business, and individuals—doctors and patients—should approach this in a logical, methodical manner. If a drug is no longer effective, upping the dose is not always the answer. Likewise, every new symptom does not warrant a different medication. A person who is on eight different drugs should probably be weaned off many of them. If they have been on the drugs for many years, one drug at a time should be reduced over a period of months.

Compounding the issue further is that many similar drugs are now available. For example, Prozac (fluoxetine) and Lexapro (escitalopram) are both SSRI second-generation antidepressants. There are various separate yet similar medications in this broad class of drugs. The upside to this is if you do not like one drug, others that address the same symptoms are there to try. The biggest mistake doctors make with antidepressants and the atypical drugs such as Risperdal (risperidone), Abilify (aripiprazole), and Seroquel (quetiapine) is giving too high a dose. Over fifty parents have told me their child did really well on a small dose of a drug but became agitated and could not sleep on a higher dose. For many people on the autism spectrum, the most effective dose of antidepressants and atypical medications is much lower than the recommended dose on the label.

A good doctor is careful in prescribing medications, changing dosage, or adding new medications to the mix. Parents need to be equally educated in understanding possible side effects, changes in behavior that signal problems, proper administration of the drug, etc. This is especially true when medications are given to children. Most medication trials are done on adults, and while the symptoms in children may mirror those in adults, their body systems are different. Little research exists on drug use in children.

Doctors and parents need to be doubly careful and consider medications only after other behavioral/educational options have failed to alleviate the symptoms. When medication is warranted, sometimes an odd combination of drugs works. (Find more information in my book *Thinking in Pictures* and the other sections in this chapter.) A good rule of thumb is that for most individuals, three or fewer drugs will usually work. This applies only to medication used to treat behavioral issues, such as anxiety, depression, or severe panic, and not to medications needed for epilepsy or other physical/biomedical conditions.

Supplement and Drug Interactions

Many parents assume that vitamins, herbs, supplements, and alternative treatments taken orally are safe because they are not "drugs." This is not true, and caution should be used with these formulations as well. Vitamins are either water-soluble or fat-soluble. Water-soluble vitamins are not stored in the body. The body metabolizes what it needs when taken and excretes the rest through the urine. These vitamins need to be replenished on a regular basis. Fat-soluble vitamins, on the other hand, are stored in the liver and fatty tissues in the body and are eliminated much more slowly. Vitamins A, D, E, and K are fat-soluble. Care should be taken in using these, since they can build up in the system and cause toxic reactions. The body systems of individuals with autism are often wired differently; their immune systems can be impaired. Parents and doctors should not automatically assume that the recommended dosage on the bottle is appropriate. Trained professionals should be consulted when using any supplement with a child or adult with autism. Herbs deserve the same cautionary measures too. While they have been used for hundreds of years, little research has been done on different combinations of herbs or different dosages used for individuals in today's society, especially when other medications are involved.

The more things used with a child—either conventional or alternative or a combination of both—the more likely a bad interaction will occur at one point. This is the primary reason to try only one medication or supplement at a time, so you can observe its effects before you add another. Some interactions are very dangerous; adjusting doses can compensate for others. One drug may block the metabolism of another. When this occurs, it may cause the same effect as a double dose of the drug because the drug is removed more slowly from the body. This can result in different reactions, ranging from sleepiness to agitation, in different individuals. Even typical food products can affect how the body processes medications, vitamins, or supplements. For instance, grapefruit juice enhances the effects of many drugs in weird ways, while orange juice does not. Some supplements act as blood thinners, and too high a dose can cause bleeding. St. John's Wort speeds up drug metabolism and may render vital drugs such as antibiotics ineffective.

I took a soy-based gel cap natural calcium supplement that had strange hormonal effects and made my post-menopausal breasts sore. Now I make sure all my calcium supplements have no soy in them. I also had a friend who drank a quart of soy milk every day and had menstrual problems. She recovered when she stopped drinking it. Soy contains plant estrogens and should be used in moderation.

Conventional medications can also have serious side effects, among them diabetes or skin rashes. The biggest side effect of the atypical class of drugs is weight gain, and sometimes it is significant. Gaining one hundred pounds while on a medication is not an acceptable side effect. For some individuals, weight gain can be controlled by either switching to a different drug or cutting back on high-glycemic carbs such as sugared drinks, white bread, and potatoes. Parents need to carefully monitor side effects and drug interactions. Doctors see patients only sporadically; parents see their kids every day. Tell your doctor *everything* you or your child is taking or any time you add something new into the mix, no matter how "safe" you deem it to be.

Biomedical Treatments

For young children under age eight, I would recommend trying some of the biomedical treatments first, before using conventional medications. Reports from parents and individuals on the spectrum indicate that the single most important biomedical treatment to try is a special diet. They are often most helpful for children who have the regressive form of autism, where they lose language at eighteen to twenty-four months.

Unfortunately, when data from many studies are pooled, the diets fail to show improvements. The problem is that autism is a broad spectrum, with many subgroups. From my own observations, the diets may work really well in about 10 percent of children who have autism. They may be most likely to be beneficial in children with digestive and bowel problems.

Special diets can be tried with individuals of all ages, not just children. Gastrointestinal problems are often more common in individuals with autism. Pain from acid reflux (heartburn) or other digestive problems may cause behavior problems. Special diets may help ease these gastrointestinal issues.

Special diets can help some children and adults with autism and have no effect on others. There are two basic types: the gluten-free, casein-free (GFCF) diet (on which you avoid wheat and dairy) and the specific carbohydrate diet (SCD). A special diet is noninvasive and, for some individuals, can bring about remarkable positive changes. However, special diets require time and attention and, in many cases, need to be implemented religiously to truly ascertain whether or not they work for an individual. Usually a trial of one to three months is all that's needed to gauge effectiveness. Some parents notice positive changes after only a few short days on the diet. Others find their child's behavior gets worse for a few days before it turns around and improvements begin. Dedication to "doing the diet" faithfully is needed once one begins. Some parents will try "a little of the diet" and find it doesn't work, when if they had done it completely, the result might have been more positive.

Critics of special diets cite the lack of scientific research to support their use with this population. Literally hundreds and hundreds of parents have reported they work, and a double-blind, placebo-controlled scientific study has been completed. It is impossible to overlook this large (and growing!) body of anecdotal support. Other critics cite the cost of special diets, having to purchase special foods that are often expensive and sometimes difficult to find locally. This doesn't have to be the case, given a little ingenuity on the part of the family. A simple, inexpensive, dairy-free and wheat-free diet could consist of rice, potatoes, whole fresh fruit, vegetables, beans, corn tortillas, nuts, eggs, beef, chicken, pork, and fish. The amount of sugar in the diet should be monitored and, in most cases, reduced. Olive oil can be used instead of casein-containing butter, and all soy products must be avoided.

In general, these special diets are healthy ways of eating. Families with a child on a special diet will find themselves eating a healthier diet and incorporating more fresh fruits and vegetables into their meals. A new study done in Australia has shown that there was more depression and anxiety when people ate a diet high in sugar and refined wheat, compared to a healthier diet of meat, fish, vegetables, fruit, and whole grains. Some examples of refined wheat products are white bread, snack cakes, waffles, and pasta. If the GFCF diet works, the child must start taking calcium supplements because he is getting no dairy products.

The specific carbohydrate diet differs in that wheat is avoided, but dairy in the form of plain, unsweetened yogurt and cheese can often be added back into the eating plan. High glycemic index carbs such as potatoes, rice, fruit juices, and most refined sugar sweets are omitted. This eating plan is similar to an Atkins diet. The glycemic index for every food can easily be looked up on the internet. Most of the bread substitutes that can be eaten on the GFCF diet should be avoided on the SCD because the glycemic index is too high. Many of these products contain lots of sugar and refined potato starch or refined rice starch. The most important carbs to reduce or eliminate are from drinks. I eat whole fruit instead of juices, and I have eliminated both regular soda and diet soda. A study published in the *Yale Journal of Biological Medicine* indicated that artificial sweeteners may contribute to weight gain.

Problems with a Limited Diet

There are some autistic individuals who have a very limited diet and eat only a few things. They should be given a high-quality multiple vitamin to prevent the old-fashioned vitamin deficiency diseases that doctors may not recognize. One young adult got scurvy due to a lack of vitamin C in his diet. His doctor did not know what it was. Vitamin C supplements cleared it up. A single high-quality multivitamin will prevent nasty vitamin deficiency diseases.

My Special Diet Experience

Neither the GFCG diet nor the SCD had a positive effect on my anxiety problems. Later in life, a gluten-free diet helped me reduce heartburn. For me, only conventional antidepressants stopped the panic attacks. At seventy-six, my immune function was getting poor, and I started getting constant urinary tract infections and yeast infections. I was constantly taking antibiotics and antifungals to control them. Today I am controlling these problems with both diet and acidophilus/bifidobacteria probiotic supplements. Dietary strategies have worked well for me to control these problems, and I no longer use antibiotics. Plain Dannon Yogurt or Chobani Yogurt helped me with the urinary tract infections and when yeast problems started.

Scientists are learning more about the complex ecosystem of bacteria in the gut. To keep my probiotics working, I rotate to a different brand every few months. This sounds crazy, but I stopped several beginning yeast infections before they became severe by eating brie or Camembert cheese. I don't eat this cheese all the time because I fear that the ecosystem in my gut may adapt to it.

I made up my own simple version of the SCD. I greatly restricted bread, potatoes, rice, pasta, and other foods with a high glycemic index. Drinks or foods full of sugar are totally avoided, since sugar feeds the growth of yeast.

To keep the glycemic index down, I eat animal protein, eggs, or fish three times a day and use healthy olive oil on my salads. My diet includes lots of vegetables, salads, whole fruit, and black beans. Animal protein is especially important at breakfast. A breakfast full of low-fat carbs made my yeast infections worse and caused me to get either headaches or light-headed before lunch. A good meat or egg breakfast with some fat in it along with fresh whole fruit makes me feel so much better. I also never put food in a blender or drink fruit juice. Eating whole fruit is beneficial because digestion is slower, which also reduces the glycemic index. My drinks are water, plain tea with lemon, coffee, and tiny amounts of wine. Dairy products are eaten in limited amounts. Restricting wheat helps, but I eat small amounts so I do not get so sensitive to wheat that I would have to worry about trace amounts. I have one word of warning. Taking most of the "big white carbs" out of my diet sometimes makes my stomach hurt. When this happens, I have a little rice with my meat, fruit, and vegetables or eat an apple. The food in my diet is not organic, and everything I need can be easily purchased at the regular grocery store. I have to be really careful about eating or drinking too many high-glycemic carbs on an empty stomach. One large glass of juice with 60 grams of carbs caused a huge yeast infection. To get the yeast back under control, I had to eat an ultra-low-carb diet for a month.

I love sweets and wine. After I got my yeast infection controlled, I found I could have very small amounts of full-fat ice cream, wine, or dark chocolate if I always ate it with a full meal. In addition to watching what I eat, I take 500 mg of vitamin C, a standard multiple vitamin, vitamin B complex, calcium with vitamin D, and an occasional omega-3. I buy all my vitamins at the regular drug store with the exception of the B complex, which is Blue Bonnet 100 from Whole Foods. I have to be careful with omega-3 because it interacts with my antidepressant, and I get nose bleeds if I take too much. The omega-3 (fish oil) supplements have many beneficial effects that are now documented by research studies. Fish oil is more effective than flax as a source of omega-3. Two research studies show that omega-3 is useful for children with autism. I get most of my omega-3s by eating salmon twice a week. Tuna should be avoided due to its high mercury content.

Today I eat a small amount of yogurt with active cultures and Solaray Multidophilus, which is an acidophilus and bifidobacteria supplement. This probiotic contains billions of the same organisms that are in yogurt. The liquid ban at airport security made traveling with yogurt in my carry-on bag impossible. Fortunately, airport stores and many hotels have either Dannon or Chobani Yogurt. I also break open the capsules and dab some of the powder on topically at the site of the yeast infection. Yeast and urinary tract infections alternate. Yeast seems to inhibit urinary tract infections. D-mannose is something you can try that has worked well for some people.

When I feel a urinary infection just starting, I stop topical application of the culture and eat some extra sugar along with a cranberry supplement. A small amount of sugar seems to boost the yeast just a little bit and stops the urinary tract infection before it starts. This only works when I feel the first twinges of an infection. If a urinary tract infection becomes established, it must be treated with antibiotics. I also take Solaray Yeast Cleanse, an herbal product for yeast infections. If I have to take antibiotics, I stop taking all herbal (plant-based) supplements because they may prevent the antibiotic from working. They are resumed the day after I get off the antibiotic.

Biomedical and Conventional Options

Our knowledge of biomedical treatments and their effect on individuals with autism is growing. Some biomedical interventions are easy and relatively inexpensive to try. Others are costly, and some, like chelation, should be approached with the utmost caution, since improper administration can result in death. Recent research indicates that hyperbaric oxygen is not effective as a treatment. The diets and omega-3 (fish oil) and other supplements such as extra B vitamins, DMG (dimethylglycine), or probiotics are noninvasive and worth trying.

The supplement creatine is showing promise for improving depression. Melatonin is often effective as a sleep aid. There is good evidence-based research to support the use of melatonin for sleep problems associated with autism. Researchers from several universities reported that parents perceived that melatonin was one of the most effective complementary treatments.

The evidence-based information on omega-3 is less clear. One meta-analysis showed that omega-3 was helpful for ADHD. I hypothesize that the lack of evidence for autism may be due to omega-3 only being helpful when the child's diet is deficient in omega-3. Studies show that a deficiency of omega-3 is associated with faulty emotional processing.

There is a need for good research on biomedical treatments, as they work differently in different autism subtypes. Until that comes about, parents should carefully weigh the pros and cons of any biomedical option and add in new biomedical interventions one at a time, to gauge effectiveness.

The *sensible* use of *both* conventional and alternative biomedical treatment has worked well for me. Each child and family is different, however, and parents should never use biomedical options or conventional medication because "everyone is doing it." I am a really practical person and know that if I am going to use an alternative method like a special diet, I have to figure out how to do that without it interfering with my work or my extensive travel schedule and without costing me a fortune. With some research and planning, parents can find ways to test out various options on their child, too.

Tips on Finding Information

It is best to base treatment decisions on well-done scientific studies that have been published in respected, peer-reviewed medical journals. This is what doctors call "evidence-based medicine." Unfortunately, the majority of options available now for treating the challenges associated with autism have no or limited evidence of this quality to support them. Parents, nonetheless, are trying these options in their search for ways to help their children. When peer-reviewed research has not been done on a particular treatment option, what's a parent to do? Valuable information can be gleaned by talking to parents, teachers, and individuals on the autism spectrum. The tip on eating meat or eggs three times a day came from a friend who had an uncontrollable yeast infection that could not be stopped with conventional medication. I trust information from sources where there is no conflict of interest with somebody trying to sell me something. This principle applies to both conventional and alternative medicine. Because a professional is an MD does not eliminate personal bias, nor less-than-ethical behavior. It is common knowledge now that doctors accept all sorts of "incentives"—including monthly bonuses—for prescribing certain drugs over others. Parents *must* become educated consumers and question, investigate, and evaluate any drug or alternative treatment recommended for their child.

Another principle I use in decision-making is that the more expensive, invasive, or hazardous a potential treatment is, the more documented proof I need that it is effective. I will try a simple dietary change based on a friend's recommendation, but I am not going to spend thousands of dollars or do something potentially hazardous because a friend said I should try it. Back in 1980 when I started taking Tofranil to control my anxiety, few doctors knew that antidepressants worked for anxiety and panic attacks. I had read about the early research in a popular magazine. My next step was to find scientific journal articles before I asked my doctor to put me on Tofranil. And even then, it was a decision we discussed and both agreed upon.

Today, finding medical information on the internet is easy. Not all of it is reliable. There is lots of rubbish and hucksters selling snake oil mixed in with the really useful information. To avoid this, you can search scientific articles on PubMed, Google Scholar, or Science Direct. To find these sites, type their names into Google. PubMed will give you free summaries of journal articles from the National Library of Medicine. Google Scholar searches scientific information and filters out most commercial websites, and Science Direct does something similar.

Another great source is Research Gate. It can lead to lots of free articles. Some of the websites where parents and patients chat can also provide useful tips and information.

When I cannot find scientific journal articles, I have a rule for evaluating some of the more exotic, expensive, or hazardous treatments. It is the three-family or three-individuals rule. I have to find three families who can convince me the treatment works after thirty minutes of detailed questioning. The first question I ask is, "Did you start another therapy such as a diet or ABA at the same time you started the treatment X?" If they say yes, I have no way of knowing that the therapy in question worked. The next part of my questioning seeks specific descriptions of behavior changes. I will not accept vague "it made them better" answers. I want specifics such as "within two weeks they went from ten words to over seventy-five words" or "tantrums went from five a day to one a week." If the family cannot provide these kinds of answers, then it is likely the beneficial effect of the therapy is wishful thinking or perhaps came about because of the placebo effect (improvement resulting from the increased attention given to the child during the treatment period). In doing this informal research of my own, I have found not just three, but numerous families and individuals who have obtained positive effects from using special diets, Irlen lenses, and some supplements. For some of the more exotic treatments, I have not been able to find three families; all I find are salespeople and often extremely costly treatments. It is important to keep an open mind in considering new biomedical options or in using conventional medications, but in the end, the adage still applies: "Buyer Beware."

Additional Reading

Adams, J.B., Audhya, T., McDonough S., et al. 2011. Effects of vitamins and mineral supplements on children and adults with autism. *BMC Pediatrics* 11:111.

Al-Bettagi, M. et al. (2023) Role of gastrointestinal health managing children with autism spectrum disorder, *World Journal of Pediatrics*, 12(4):171-196.

Ammingen, G.P. et al. 2007. Omega-3 fatty acid supplementation in children with autism: A double-blind randomized, placebo-controlled pilot study. *Biological Psychiatry* 61: 551-553.

Bloch, M.H., Qawasm, A. 2011. Omega-3 fatty acids supplementation for the children with attention deficient/hyperactivity disorders symptomatology: systematic review and meta-analysis. *Journal American Academy of Child and Adolescent Psychiatry.* 50: 991-1000.

Bock, K., and C. Stauth. 2007. *Healing the New Childhood Epidemics: Autism, AHA, Asthma, and Allergies.* New York: Ballantine Books.

Doyle, B. 2007. Prescription for success: Considerations in the use of medications to change the behavior of children or adults with ASD. *Autism Asperger's Digest*, July-August 2007: 18-23.

Gow, R.V., Sumich A., Vallea-Tourangaav F, et al. 2013. Omega-3 fatty ac- ids are related to abnormal emotion processing in adolescent boys with attention deficit hyperactivity disorder. *Prostaglandins Leukotrienes and Essential Fatty Acids (PLEFA)* 88: 419-429.

Gow, R.V., Vallea-Tourangaav F., Crawford, M. A., et al. 2013. Omega-3 fatty acids are inversely related to callous unemotional traits in adolescent boys with ADHD. *Prostaglandins Leukotrienes and Essential Fatty Acids (PLEFA)* 88: 411416.

Grandin, T. 2006. *Thinking in Pictures* (Expanded Edition). New York: Vintage/Random House.

Knivsberg, A.M., K.L. Reichelt, T. Hoien, and M. Nodland. 2002. A randomized, controlled study of dietary intervention in autistic syndromes. *Nutritional Neuroscience* 5: 251-261.

Lindsay, R., and M.G. Aman. 2003. Pharmacologic therapies and treatment for autism. *Pediatric Annals* 32: 671-676.

Lespérance F., Frasure-Smith N., St-André E., et al. 20112010. The efficacy of omega-3 supplementation for major depression: a randomized con- trolled trial. *Journal of Clinical Psychiatry*. 72: 1054-1062.

Mertz, G., and E. Bazelon. 2007. When less may be more: Searching for the optimal medication dosage. *Autism Asperger's Digest*, November-December 2007: 52-55.

Pierluigi P., Mateo R., Enzo E. et al. 2013. Randomized placebo-controlled trials of Omega-3 polysaturated fatty acids for psychiatric disorder. A review of current literature. *Current Drug Discovery Technologies* 10: 245- 25.

Vandan, P. et al. (2023) Autism spectrum disorder and complementary integrative medicine, Child Adolescent Psychiatry Clinic of North America, 32(2):469-194.

Yang, Q. (2010) Gain weight by "going on a diet?" Artificial sweeteners and the neurobiology of sugar craving, *Yale Journal of Biological Medicine*, 83(2):101-108.

Yoon L. I., Kim T. S., Hwang J., et al. 2012. A randomized double-blind placebo-controlled trial of oral creatine monohydrate augmentation for enhanced response to a selective reuptake inhibitor in women with major depressive disorders. *American Journal of Psychiatry*. 169: 937-945.

Zhang, J., Mayton, M. R., Wheeler, J. J. 2013. Effectiveness of gluten-free and casein-free diets for individuals with autism spectrum disorders: an evidence-based research synthesis. *Education and Training in Autism and Developmental Disabilities*. 48: 276-287.

I like the "à la carte" approach. Use a few items from both sectors of medicine (alternative and conventional) that really work for you; discontinue items that do not.

ALTERNATIVE VERSUS CONVENTIONAL MEDICINE

Many people make the mistake of taking sides in the debate between conventional medications and alternative treatments, such as special diets or vitamin supplements.

Being a practical person, I think the best approach is to pick the item(s) from each that work best for you or your child. One of the most problematic mistakes specialists in the autism field can make is becoming too wedded to their favorite theory. The debate over the benefits of conventional medication versus so-called "natural" or "biomedical" treatments has turned into a hotly contested issue. I advise you to ignore all the rhetoric and logically figure out what works for your child. The way I see it, this is the truly scientific approach to helping your child. Here's a good rule to follow: if a treatment is either very expensive or possibly dangerous, then it should only be utilized if it is supported by rigorous scientific studies.

CBD Oil (Cannabidiol)

There is great interest now in CBD oil. This is a derivative of marijuana or hemp that has the THC removed, preventing it from making you high. It is legal in many (but not all) states in the US, and in several countries globally.

Cannabidiol has been found to be effective in treating severe uncontrollable epileptic seizures, and there is increasing evidence that it may be helpful for both autism and ADHD. Some people on the autism spectrum even smoke marijuana to relieve their anxiety. This should be avoided in children and teenagers, as there is evidence that the THC in marijuana may be very bad for the developing brain. The brain does not become fully developed until age twenty-five, so until this age, it is recommended to avoid marijuana and products that contain high amounts of THC. A big literature search by Canadian researchers clearly shows that adolescents should avoid cannabis. There was an increase in psychosis. The cannabis today contains a much greater amount of THC. It is also never recommended to consume CBD oil or any other oil-based substance through a vape pen. This can cause severe, permanent lung damage.

First-Person Reports on Combining Conventional and Alternative Methods

I have observed individuals who responded very well to a combination of conventional medicine and alternative treatments. The most famous case is that of Donna Williams, an individual with autism and author of the books *Nobody Nowhere* and *Somebody Somewhere*. Over the years, I have observed Donna at several conferences. During her early years, she could not tolerate the noise and clapping at a large conference.

When I first talked to Donna, she told me that Irlen lenses and a gluten- and casein-free (GFCF) diet helped reduce her severe sensory problems. At that time, Donna was an avid believer in the use of alternative methods instead of conventional medications.

At the 2002 World Autism Conference in Australia, Donna told the audience that she had added a tiny dose, just one-quarter of a milligram, of risperidone to her daily regime. The combination of a small dose of medicine along with the special diet really brought about additional positive changes for her. One case report showed that risperidone may reduce sound sensitivity, which may explain why Donna can now tolerate large, noisy places.

I know another person who was helped greatly by a combination of Irlen lenses, the GFCF diet, and sertraline. Sertraline was used initially, and the lenses were added a year later. The glasses really helped her organize her writing and do better at her schoolwork. This was not the placebo effect because, initially, she thought that colored glasses were "stupid." Today, she loves them. About a year after the glasses were introduced, she implemented the GFCF diet, resulting in further improvements. Eventually, while she remained strictly gluten-free, she has been able to add dairy products back into her diet. Like Donna, this woman continues to use conventional medicine, diet, and Irlen lenses successfully.

Sensible Approach

There is such a thing as going overboard: taking every supplement in the health food store, for example, would be really foolish. I like the "à la carte" approach. Use a few items from both sectors of medicine that really work for you; discontinue the items that do not. For me, the GFCF diet has no effect on my anxiety, but it prevents a lightheaded, dizzy sensation because I eat some animal protein every day. I also take conventional antidepressant medication. It works really well for me, and I describe its effects in my book *Thinking in Pictures*.

I have found a combination that works well for me. With some experimentation, you can find what works best for you or your child, too. It's worth the effort.

Supplements and Diets

Scientific evidence has started to corroborate that there are specific conditions where natural treatments are effective. Dr. Dienke Bos in the Netherlands has found that dietary omega-3 fatty acids have improved ADHD symptoms. A review of some of the new research on omega-3 indicated a small, positive effect on hyperactivity. There is also some new evidence that omega-3 oils may help treat major depression in adults, as some cases suggest depression can be linked to low-grade inflammation. Fish oil and other anti-inflammatory drugs, such as aspirin and celecoxib, are sometimes helpful. Many parents have reported that the casein- and gluten-free diet is helpful. In some children, going off the diet caused a really bad reaction. There is a subgroup of individuals who respond really well. One study showed that a modified ketogenic diet with MCT (coconut) oil had some benefits, too. Common problems for many children and adults with autism include difficulty sleeping and gastrointestinal (GI) problems. A randomized trial of a sustained-release melatonin improved sleep, and three new studies showed that probiotics may be helpful in individuals with GI issues.

Additional Reading

Al-Bettig, M. et al. (2023) Role of gastrointestinal health in managing children with autism spectrum disorder, *World Journal of Clinical Pediatrics*, 12(4):171-196.

Appleton, Katherine M, Hannah M Sallis, Rachel Perry, Andrew R Ness, and Rachel Churchill. 2015. "Omega 3 Fatty Acids for Depression in Adults." Cochrane Database of Systematic Reviews. https://doi.org/10.1002/14651858. CD004692.pub4.

Arteaga-Henriquez, G. et al. (2019) Low grade inflammation as a predictor of antidepressant and anti-inflammatory therapy response in MDD (major depressive disorder), Patients: A systematic Review of the Literature, *Frontiers in Psychiatry*, 10:458.

Baur, I. et al., 2014. Does omega-3 fatty acid supplementation enhance neural efficiency? A review of the literature, *Human Psychopharmacology*, 29:8-18.

Banchel, D.A. et al. (2019) Oral cannabidiol (CBD) use in children with autism spectrum disorder to treat co-morbidities, *Frontiers in Pharmacology*, doi:10.3389/fphar.2018.0151.

Cheng, Y.S. et al. (2017) Supplementation with Omega 3 fatty acids may improve hyperactivity, lethargy and stereotypy in children with autism spectrum disorder: A meta-analysis of randomized controlled trials, *Neuropsychiatry Disorders Treatment*, 13:2531-2543.

Cooper, R.E. et al. (2017) Cannabinoids (CBD) in attention-deficit/hyperactivity disorder: A randomized controlled trial, *European Pharmacology*, 27:795-808.

Devinsky, O. et al. (2017) Trial of cannabidiol (CBD) for drug-resistant seizures in Dravet syndrome, *New England Journal of Medicine*, 376:2011- 2020.

Eaton, W.E. (2015) Improvement in psychotic symptoms after a gluten-free diet in a boy with complex autoimmune illness, *American Journal of Psychiatry*, 172:219-221.

Ghanizadeh, A. (2009) Does risperidone improve hyperacusis in children with autism? *Pharmacology Bulletin* 42:108-110.

Granpeesheh, D. et al. (2010) controlled evaluation of the effects of hyperbaric oxygen therapy on the behavior of 16 children with autism spectrum disorders, *Journal of Autism and Developmental Disorders* EPUB).

Infante, M. et al. (2018) Omega 3-PUFAs and Vitamin D co-supplementation as a safe-effective therapeutic approach for core symptoms of autism spectrum disorder: Case report and literature review, *Nutritional Neuroscience*, December 13, 2018.

Kaur, N. et al. (2021) Variations of cannabis-related adverse mental health and addiction outcomes across adolescence and adulthood, A scoping review, *Frontiers in Psychiatry*, 10.13973988.

Lee, R.W. et al. (2018) A modified ketogenic gluten free diet with MCT (coconut oil) improves behavior in children with autism spectrum disorder, *Physiology and Behavior*, 188:205-211.

Lui, J. et al. (2019) Probiotic therapy for treating behavioral and gastro- intestinal symptoms in autism spectrum disorder: A systematic review of clinical trials, *Current Medical Science*, 39:173-184.

Lui, Y.W. et al. (2019) Effects of lactobacillus plantarum PS128 on children with autism spectrum disorder in Taiwan: A randomized double-blind placebo-controlled trial, *Nutrients* 11(4):820.

Maris, A. et al. (2018) Melatonin for insomnia in patients with autism, *Child Adolescent Psychopharmacology*, 28:699-710.

Mulloy, A. et al. (2010) Gluten free and casein free diets in the treatment of autism spectrum disorder, *Research in Autism Spectrum Disorders*, 4:328-339.

Navarro, F. et al. (2016) Can probiotics benefit children with autism spectrum disorder? *World Journal of Gastroenterology*, 22:10093-10102.

Orr, C. et al. (2019) Gray matter volume differences with extremely low levels of cannabis use in adolescents, *Journal of Neuroscience* doi:10.1523/ jneurosci.3375-17.2018.

Parrella, N.F. et al. (2023) A systematic review of cannabidiol (CBD) trials in neurodevelopmental disorders. *Pharmocology Biochemstry of Behavior*, 173607.

Polag, S. et al. (2019) Cannabidiol (CBD) as a suggested candidate for treatment of autism spectrum disorder, *Progress in Neuro-Psychopharmacology and Biological Psychiatry*, 89:90-96.

Posar, A. and Viscotti, P. (2018) Omega 3 supplementation in autism spectrum disorder: A still open question, *Journal of Pediatric Neuroscience*, 11:225-227.

Rucklidge, J.J. (2014) Vitamin-mineral treatment of attention deficit hyperactivity disorder in adults: A double-blind study randomized placebo-controlled trial, *BJ Psych* doi: 10.1192/bjp.bp.113.132.

Sakulchit, T. et al. (2017) Hyperbaric oxygen therapy for children with autism spectrum disorder, CFP-MFC, *The Official Journal of the College of Family Physicians in Canada*, 63:446-448 (Not recommended).

Schleider, L.B.L. et al. (2019) Real life experience of medical cannabidiol (CBD) treatment of autism: Analysis of safety and efficiency, *Scientific Reports* (Nature) 200.

Shattock, P. and P. Whiteley (2000) *The Sunderland Protocol: A logical sequencing of biomedical intervention for the treatment of autism and related disorders*, Autism Research Unit, University of Sunderland, UK.

Zhang, W.F. et al. (2010) Extract of ginkgo biloba treatment for tardive dyskinesia in schizophrenics: A randomized double-blind, placebo-controlled trial, *Journal of Clinical Psychiatry*, (pub).

Before a medication or supplement is used, you have to determine what is causing a behavior problem. Is it behavioral, or is it medical?

AUTISM MEDICAL UPDATE

The new information on supplements and CBD is on pages 60-61. In this section, I will cover some of the most recent information on other medically related topics. Anxiety is a major problem for many teens and adults with autism. Reports from both parents and counselors indicate that anxiety, and sometimes panic attacks, prevent the individual from engaging in activities. When I was in my twenties, I was terrified of both public speaking and airplanes. To get comfortable with public speaking, I just had to do it. Having really good slides to illustrate my talk was also extremely helpful. To get over the fear of flying, I made aviation interesting. Flying in the cockpit of a large plane carrying cattle switched aircrafts from "scary" to "interesting."

In many of my writings, such as my book *Thinking in Pictures*, I discussed how a low dose of antidepressants saved me from crippling panic attacks. There is an excellent review of medications for anxiety at the Kennedy Krieger Institute (www.iamcommunity.org). In this review, they discuss problems with over-activation caused by antidepressants. Unfortunately, they do not discuss the use of lower doses. If you try an antidepressant and it causes agitation or insomnia, the dose must be reduced. I also found a good open-access scientific article on pharmacological therapies for autism by Dr. D. W. Coleman in the *Journal of Child and Adolescent Psychopharmacology* (see Additional Reading list). There are some individuals who are taking too many medications. Fifty percent of adults with autism in the Medicaid program were on six or more drugs. It is likely that they are overmedicated. In a paper by Rini Votira at West Virginia University, there is a good discussion of the serious side effects of atypical drugs such as risperidone and Abilify. There is also some exciting new research on treatment-resistant depression. There are some cases where subclinical low thyroid hormone levels may be one reason. Parents, teachers, and doctors need to think logically about the use of medications. Way too many drugs are given to young children, and they may have unknown effects on the developing brain. When a medication is introduced, it should have an obvious beneficial effect.

Determining the Cause of Behavior Problems

There are several different reasons why individuals with autism or other developmental problems have meltdowns. The first step is to determine if the problem is behavioral or medical. Below are the major causes of meltdowns:

- *Behavioral:* Child has a tantrum when he/she does not get what they want.

- *Behavioral:* Frustration because of an inability to communicate. Give the child a method to communicate their needs. Providing a method for a nonverbal individual to communicate will prevent many behavior problems.

- *Behavioral:* An attempt to get out of doing something he/she does not want to do.

- *Medical:* Extreme sensory oversensitivity, meltdowns, or violent behavior in teenagers and adults in response to loud noise or sensory overload. Try a low dose of an atypical antipsychotic such as risperidone, which is approved by the FDA for irritability associated with autism. Due to severe side effects, try to avoid use in young children.

- *Medical:* There are hidden painful medical problems a nonverbal child or adult cannot tell you about. Gastrointestinal issues such as constipation or heartburn are common causes. You must also rule out yeast infections, urinary tract infections, toothaches, and earaches.

- *Medical:* Psycho-motor epilepsy—An antiseizure or epileptic drug may be effective when a tantrum suddenly occurs when there is no reason for it. The individual may scream or hit without warning. Suspect psycho-motor epilepsy if a meltdown occurs when the individual is in a quiet place just relaxing. These seizures are extremely difficult to diagnose. A trial of an anticonvulsant drug may work. If it works, it will be obvious. A large survey of medication for autism gave high rankings to lamotrigine (Lamictal) and oxcarbazepine (Trileptal) as good anticonvulsants (epilepsy drugs).

- *Medical:* Hot and sweaty rage—There are some children and adults with whom blood pressure medications may be really helpful. A book titled *Hope for the Violently Aggressive Child* may provide useful recommendations.

Findings about Melatonin

A randomized controlled trial showed that melatonin is effective in helping individuals with autism with sleep problems. Sometimes parents prefer to use natural supplements because they are concerned about bad side effects with conventional medications. These are real and legitimate concerns. However, there are some situations where a medication may be beneficial to the brain. Long-term use of citalopram (Celexa), an SSRI antidepressant, may help prevent Alzheimer's. This medication is often used to treat anxiety.

Causes of Autism

There is a lot of speculation on the causes of autism. Genetics are a major factor in the cause of autism, as there are many different genes that are involved with brain development that contribute to autism. Genomic testing indicates that genes that contribute to autism occur in both humans and animals. A question I often get asked is: has autism increased?

Some of the increase, I think, is due to too much screen time and a lack of formal social skills training. Most children of my generation received lots of social skills training as a normal parenting practice. If a person has only a slight tendency to be socially aloof, that tendency may increase if their activities become more solitary. Both the environment and genetics are important. Many children today have no grit or persistence because they are not allowed to figure things out by themselves. An interesting experiment with rats showed that they were more persistent and successful in getting food out of a puzzle box if they had to forage for their food instead of just having it given to them. Rats that had to dig in piles of sawdust to get treats were better problem solvers than rats that had them scattered on the floor. Children need to be given more time to explore and figure out things themselves.

Additional Reading

Ankenman, R. (2014) *Hope for the Violently Aggressive Child: New Diagnoses and Treatments That Work*, Future Horizons, Arlington, Texas.

Bardi, M. et al. (2012) Behavioral training and predisposed coping strategies interact to influence resilience in male Long-Evans rats: Implications for depression, *Stress*, 15(3):306-317.

Bartels, C. et al. (2018) Impact of SSRI therapy on risk of conversion from mild cognitive impairment to Alzheimer's Dementia in individuals with previous depression, *American Journal of Psychiatry*, 175(3):232-241.

Cohen, B.M. et al. (2018) Antidepressant resistant depression in patients with co-morbid subclinical hypothyroidism or near normal TSH levels, *American Journal of Psychiatry*, 175(7):598-604.

Coleman, D.M. et al. (2019) Rating of the effectiveness of 26 psychiatric medications and seizure medications for Autism Spectrum Disorder: Results of National Survey, *Journal of Child and Adolescent Psychopharmacology*, 29(2).

Healings, J.A. et.al. (2024) Minimally verbal individuals with autism spectrum disorder/intellectual disability and behavior challenges: can strategies with psychiatric treatment help? *Disabilities*, 412, 277-289.

LeCleve, S. et al. (2015) Pharmacological treatments for autism spectrum disorder: A review, *P&T* 40(6):389-397.

Maras, A. et al. (2018) Melatonin for insomnia in patients with autism, *Child and Adolescent Psychopharmacology* 28(10): 699-710.

Reser, J.E. (2014) Solitary mammals as a model for autism, *Journal of Comparative Psychology*, 128(1):99-113.

Shpigler, H.Y. et al. (2017) Deep evolutionary conservation of autism-related genes, *PNAS* 114(36): 9653-9658.

Sikela, J.M. et al. (2014) Genomic Trade-offs - Are autism and schizophrenia the steep price of the human brain? *Human Genetics* 137(1):1-13.

VanDana, P. et al. (2023) Autism spectrum disorder and complementary integrative medicine, *Clinical Adolescent Psychiatry*, Clinics of North America 32(2):469-494.

Vohra, R. et al. (2016) Prescription drug use and polypharmacy among Medicaid-enrolled adults with autism: A retrospective cross-sectional analysis, Drugs Real World Outcomes, *Springer* 3(4):409-425.

VonHoldt, B.W. et al. (2017) Structural variants in genes associated with human Williams-Beuren Syndrome underlie stereotypical hypersociability in domestic dogs, *Science Advances* 3(7)@1700398.

All medications have risks. When making decisions about medication usage, the benefits should clearly—not marginally—outweigh the risks.

MEDICATION USAGE: RISK VERSUS BENEFIT DECISIONS

There has been much publicity lately about the hazards associated with certain medications such as antidepressants and pain-relieving drugs for arthritis. It has raised concern among parents whose children already use medications, and has made more ardent skeptics of those who already hesitate to use drugs with their child.

All medications have risks. When making decisions about medication usage, the benefits should clearly—not marginally—outweigh the risks. Common sense dictates that drugs with a higher risk of bad side effects should be used more carefully than drugs with a low risk. A reasonable approach is to try drugs with a lower risk of side effects first.

To approach medication decision-making in a logical manner, it is best to adhere to the following three principles. These principles assume that non-drug approaches were tried *first* and proved unsuccessful in alleviating the challenge. A child should *not* be given medication as the first course of treatment when presenting behavioral challenges. Exhaust other treatments first.

A review of the literature indicated that children may have more adverse drug effects when compared with adults.

- Try one medication at a time so you can judge its effect. Do not change educational programs or diet at the same time as a new drug is tried. Allow a few weeks to a month between starting a medication and changing some other part of the individual's program. Keeping a journal of the child's behaviors, demeanor, and levels of activity can be helpful in spotting possible side effects and/or assessing the degree of improvement, if any.

- An effective medication should have an *obvious beneficial effect*. Giving a child a powerful drug that renders him only slightly less hyper would probably not be worth the risk. A drug that just takes the edge off his hyperactivity but makes him very lethargic would be equally bad. I am really concerned about the growing number of powerful drugs being prescribed to young children. In little kids, I recommend trying one of the special diets and omega-3 (fish oil) supplements first, before giving the child powerful drugs.

- If an individual has been on a medication that is working really well, it is usually not worth the risk to change it for a new medication. Newer is not always better. Pharmaceutical companies promote their new drugs while they still have patents. After a drug goes generic, they no longer promote it. However, many of the older generic drugs are very effective and cheap. Just use care when switching brands of generics. Find a brand that works well and stay with it. The way the pills are manufactured may affect how fast they dissolve, which may change the way the drug works. This is especially a problem with slow time-release drugs.

To make good decisions, parents need to know all the risks involved with the major classes of medications. The following section summarizes the uses and risks associated with the six most commonly used medications.

1. *Antidepressants:* (both SSRIs—selective serotonin reuptake inhibitors such as Prozac—and older tricyclics): When used to treat anxiety, these drugs should be given at lower doses to people on the spectrum than to the general population. Some individuals with autism need only one-quarter to one-half the normal starter dose. Giving too high a dose of an antidepressant causes many problems, such as insomnia and agitation. The correct low dose can have very positive effects. The reactions to a dose that is too high may be severe, and they will usually start within one week after starting the drug. If the symptoms occur, the drug must be either stopped immediately or given at a much lower dose. Researchers at the University of Kansas Medical Center found that low doses of the old generic ami-triptyline were helpful. I know many design professionals who take Prozac, and they have done some of their best work while taking it.

However, I have heard several complaints about memory problems with Paxil (paroxetine). Prozac (fluoxetine), Zoloft (sertraline), or Lexapro (escitalopram) would probably be better choices. In a meta-analysis, Prozac had the best evidence for use in individuals with autism when compared to other SSRIs. However, if you are taking Paxil and doing well, it would prob-ably be best to keep taking it. There are many new antidepressants on the market. Usually, they have no advantages compared to older drugs. They do, however, have the disadvantage of being much more expensive.

Antidepressants work really well for anxiety, panic attacks, obsessive-compulsive disorder (OCD), social anxiety, and racing thoughts. Most antidepressants have a "black box" warning of a slightly increased risk of suicidal thinking during the early period of use—the first eight weeks on the drug. Doctors usually prefer to try SSRIs first because they are safer. Tricyclics can cause heart problems in some susceptible individuals. Pro-zac might be less likely to trigger suicidal thoughts.

2. **Atypicals:** Some examples are Risperdal (risperidone), Seroquel (quetiapine), and Abilify (aripiprazole). The FDA is very specific and states that they are approved for irritability associated with autism. The author speculates that the irritability may have a partial sensory basis. The side effects of these drugs are high. They include weight gain, increased risk for diabetes, and tardive dyskinesia (Parkinson's shakes). Tardive dyskinesia sometimes causes permanent damage that may continue after the medication is stopped.

One study showed 15 percent of children treated with Abilify got tremors or other neurological problems. Discussions with families indicate that in young children, tardive dyskinesia may occur after one year of treatment. There is no black-box warning on the labels of these drugs, but the long-term risks are actually greater than those associated with antidepressants. Gaining one hundred pounds can seriously compromise health, impair mobility, and contribute to social ostracism and low self-esteem. The risks continue and tend to get worse the longer the drug is taken. Low doses of atypicals should be used.

These drugs are effective for controlling very severe aggression in older children and adults. Behavioral interventions should be used first before employing atypicals to control aggression. The balance between risk versus benefit favors using the atypicals for individuals with severe symptoms. For those with milder symptoms, the risks are too high.

Similarly, powerful drugs in the atypical class should not be used as sleep aids or for attention problems because they have too many severe side effects.

3. **Stimulants:** Some examples are Ritalin (methylphenidate) and Adderall (a combination of dextroamphetamine and amphetamine). These drugs

are normally prescribed for children and adults with ADHD. Stimulants usually make children with autism who have had a speech delay worse. However, they often improve individuals with mild autism where there is no speech delay. Compared to the atypicals, stimulants have fewer long-term side effects, but they should be avoided in individuals who have either diagnosed or suspected heart problems. The effects of stimulants are immediate and will become obvious after one or two doses. Other types of medicines require several weeks or more to evaluate.

4. **Anticonvulsants:** These drugs were originally developed for treating epilepsy and seizures. They are also very effective for controlling aggression and stabilizing mood. Anticonvulsants are likely to be effective if aggression starts suddenly, almost like flicking a light switch. The rage may appear to come "out of the blue," with little or no provocation. It may be triggered by a tiny seizure activity that is difficult to detect unless a sleeping electroencephalogram is performed with no sedatives. This test is very difficult to do for many children or adults with autism.

Therefore, a careful trial of an anticonvulsant may be a good choice, especially if epileptic-type activity is suspected. Risperdal or one of the other atypicals may work better for aggression that is more directed at certain people. Mark Goodman, a psychopharmacologist in Kansas, reports that Lamictal (lamotrigine) is often very effective for aggression in autistic adolescents. This is the stage of development where seizures sometimes occur in autism. Other anticonvulsants that often work well are Topamax (topiramate) and Depakote (divalproex sodium).

The main disadvantage of anticonvulsants is that blood tests have to be done to make sure they are not damaging the liver in susceptible individuals. If a skin rash develops within six months after starting an anticonvulsant, the drug must be stopped immediately. Most problems with rashes occur in the first two to eight weeks. If the person continues to take the drug, the rash can be fatal. Many individuals tolerate anticonvulsants really well, provided they have no liver or rash problems within the first year of taking these drugs. Careful monitoring will prevent dangerous side effects because the person can be taken off the drug before it causes permanent damage.

In one meta-analysis of anticonvulsants, researchers concluded that they did not work for autism. The problem with an autism diagnosis is that it is not precise like a diagnosis for tuberculosis. However, anticonvulsants may work if the individual also has some form of epileptic activity in the brain in addition to a diagnosis of autism. Anticonvulsants are approved by the FDA for treating epilepsy and for mood stabilization. I have suggested that many families who have a child with severe aggression consult with a neurologist who is skilled at treating atypical types of epilepsy. Sometimes, this has good results.

5. **Blood pressure medications:** This class of drugs was originally developed for treating high blood pressure. They have strong antianxiety and calming properties. I know design professionals who had terrible problems with anxiety and drug addiction who completely got their lives turned around by taking a low dose of Prozac along with the beta-blocker propranolol. Propranolol is an old generic that is being rediscovered. The military is doing research with propranolol and prazosin as treatment for post-traumatic stress disorder. They block the huge fear response that veterans experience during a flashback and help stop nightmares. Propranolol may help control rage in nonverbal individuals who are hot and sweaty and often sound like they are out of breath. Dr. Ralph Ankenman has a book titled *Hope for the*

Violently Aggressive Child. This book describes the use of both beta- and alpha-blocking blood pressure medicines to control rages. Other blood pressure medications may also be helpful for calming or helping a child get to sleep. Catapres (clonidine) works well as a sleep aid. Blood pressure medications have fewer long-term side effects compared to the atypicals such as Risperdal or Abilify. Since they are blood pressure pills, they could cause fainting if the person's blood pressure gets too low. When any blood pressure medication is first started, individuals should avoid driving until they know how they will react to the medication.

6. **Benzodiazepines:** These medications are used for anxiety, but they have many disadvantages. They have huge abuse potential, and getting off the drug may be very difficult to do once started.

Some of the most common ones are Xanax (alprazolam), Valium (diazepam), and Klonopin (clonazepam). Usually an antidepressant such as Prozac (fluoxetine) or Zoloft (sertraline), or a blood pressure medication is better for long-term management of anxiety. Dr. John Ratey at Harvard University usually avoids benzodiazepines when treating individuals on the autism spectrum.

Old Versus New

Many new atypicals and antidepressants are coming on the market all the time. Some of these have minor advantages compared to older drugs. Many of them are slight chemical modifications of older drugs. Often the older drugs will work just as well and are available in cheap generics. At the time of the second revision of this chapter, there were no totally new types of conventional pharmaceuticals on the market or in the research pipeline awaiting FDA approval.

Today there are effective generic drugs available for all classes of conventional pharmaceuticals used in the treatment of individuals with autism.

In terms of real risk, the antidepressants and blood pressure medications are safer for long-term health. However, there are some situations where the benefits of Risperdal far outweigh the risk. It is a very effective drug for controlling rage. If it enables a teenager to attend school, live in a group home, or have enough self-control to learn other cognitive forms of behavior management, it would be worth the risk.

Parents must logically assess the risk-benefit ratio when contemplating any form of medication usage with their child. Discuss the medication thoroughly with the child's doctor. Ask the doctor to provide you with a list of possible side effects of the medication. Do some research of your own on the internet to determine how widely and/or effectively the medication has been used with people with autism. This is especially true when medication is suggested for use with younger children. Both doctors and parents must avoid increasing drug doses or adding another medication every time there is a crisis. I have talked to parents whose child was taking eight different medications, and the child was a sedated zombie.

When medications are used carefully and conservatively, they can help normalize function. When medications are just thrown at problems without using logical thinking, the child can be so drugged that he or she may not be able to function.

Novel Effective Uses for Old Medications

Dr. Alexander Kolevzon at Mount Sinai Hospital in New York uses either Prozac or Zoloft for anxiety, and he has patients where extended-release guanfacine (Tenex, Intuniv) or atomoxetine (Strattera) also have been effective for anxiety. Both of these drugs are commonly used for ADHD. Guanfacine is a blood pressure medication, and atomoxetine is similar to antidepressants. Guanfacine is marketed as either a blood pressure medication or an ADHD treatment under different names. There are old, safe drugs that have been given new uses. Dr. Theodore Henderson, another physician who treats autism is using the drug I take, desipramine, for anxiety. It worked in 80 percent of his patients.

Additional Reading

Aishworiya, R. et al. (2022) An update on psychopharmacological treatment of autism spectrum disorder, *Neurotherapeutics*, 19(1):248-262 (Open Access).

Ankenman, R. 2011. Hope for the Violently Aggressive Child. Future Horizons, Arlington, TX

Arnold, L.E. et al. 2010. Moderators, mediators, and other predictors of risperidone response in children with autistic disorder and irritability. *Journal of Child and Adolescent Psychopharmacology* 20: 83-93.

Aull E. 2014. *The Parent's Guide to the Medical World of Autism*, Future Horizons, Inc., Arlington, TX

Beversdorf, D.Q. et al. 2008. Effect of propranolol on verbal problem-solving in autism spectrum disorder. *Neurocase* 14: 378-383.

Bhatti, L., Thome, A., Smith, P.O., et al. 2013. A retrospective study of Amitriptyline with autism spectrum disorders. *Journal of Autism and Developmental Disorders* 43: 1017–1027.

Brunssen, W.L., and Waldrop, J. 2009. Review of the evidence for treatment of children with autism with selective serotonin reuptake inhibitors. *Journal of Specialist Pediatric Nursing* 14: 183-191.

Chavez, B., Chavez-Brown, M., Sopko, M.A., and Rey, J.A. 2007. Atypical antipsychotics in children with pervasive developmental disorders. *Pediatric Drugs* 9: 249-166.

Davies, C. et al. (2023) Pharmacological treatments in autism spectrum disorder: A narrative review, *Journal of Psychopathology*, DOI:10.3148/2284-0249-N251.

Ducrocq, V.G. 2003. Immediate treatment with propranolol decreases post-traumatic stress disorder two months after trauma. *Biological Psychiatry* 54: 947-949.

Fung, L.K., Chanal, L., Libove, R.A., et al. 2012. A retrospective review of effectiveness of aripiprazole in the treatment of sensory abnormalities in autism. *Journal of Child and Adolescent Psychopharmacology* 22: 245- 248.

Haspel, T. 1995. Beta-blockers and the treatment of aggression. *Harvard Review of Psychiatry* 2: 274-281.

Lohr, D.W., Honaker, J. 2013. Atypical antipsychotics for treatment of disruptive behavior. *Pediatric Annals* 42:72-77.

McDougle, J., Sigler, K.A., Erickson, C.A., and Posey, D.J. 2008. Atypical antipsychotics in children and adolescents with autism and other developmental disorders. *Journal of Clinical Psychiatry* 67, Supplement 4: 15-20.

Mehi-Madona, L. et al. 2010. Micronutrients versus standard medication management in autism: A naturalistic case-control study. *Journal of Child and Adolescent Psychopharmacology* 20: 95-103.

Owen, M.R., Manos, R., Mankoski, R., et al. 2011. Safety and tolerability of aripiprazole for irritability in pediatric patients with autistic disorder. *Journal of Clinical Psychiatry* 72: 1270-1276.

Parikh, M.S., Kolevzon, A., and Hollander, E. 2008. Psychopharmacology of aggression in children and adults with autism: A critical review of efficacy and tolerability. *Journal of Child and Adolescent Psychopharmacology* 18: 157-178.

Possy, D. J. et al. 2008. Antipsychotics and the treatment of autism. *Journal of Clinical Investigation* 118: 6-14.

Stachnik, J.M. and Nunn-Thompson, C. 2007. Use of atypical antipsychotics in the treatment of autistic disorder. *Annals of Pharmacotherapy* 41: 626-634.

When I go out to dinner with people older than forty and talk about tinnitus, I've discovered that many people have it, and it is undiagnosed. They have either tinnitus or dizzy spells.

MY TREATMENT FOR RINGING IN THE EARS

In my late fifties, I got Ménière's disease. This is an autoimmune disorder that can cause tinnitus (ringing in the ears), deafness, and dizziness. It was really scary because I was rapidly going deaf in one ear and the ringing sound was driving me crazy. Fortunately, I never had any problems with becoming dizzy. My first symptoms were ringing in the ears, and within months, I had lost so much hearing in one ear that I could no longer use the phone. I was terrified that my other ear would go deaf. The first specialist I went to sold lots of hearing aids and was going to let me go deaf. A different doctor got the acute phase stopped with the steroid drug prednisone. Fortunately, some of my hearing in the one affected ear returned.

The ringing in my ears was so bad I could not sleep. It sounded like constant cicadas and a continuous low-pitched foghorn. Searching the internet, I found some clues for training my brain to ignore the tinnitus, which came from the cochlea (inner ear) that had been damaged by the autoimmune attack. (An autoimmune disorder is a condition that occurs when the immune system mistakenly attacks and destroys healthy body tissue.)

One website said nature sounds help, so I went to Barnes & Noble and purchased every new-age CD they had. I tried playing many different CDs at night to mask the dreadful din in my ear, yet I still had trouble sleeping. Today you can use music streaming services. I got an important clue from another website that said, "Use of music and other sounds for relieving tinnitus is 'habituation' and not 'masking.'" So I started playing the CDs at night very softly so I had to strain to hear them. This technique resulted in them working better because I had to concentrate on hearing them. I found one CD that really worked. When I put this CD on very softly, I could tune the tinnitus out.

The Brain Cannot Listen to Three Things at Once

I had to figure out why this CD worked. It was a CD that had a combination of babbling brooks with music and intermittent birds chirping. It was the combination of the intermittent high-pitched sounds and the continuous lower-pitched water sounds that made it effective. This worked because my brain cannot pay attention to three things at once. The three things were the tinnitus, birds chirping, and wave sounds. Other combinations of sounds that worked were a wave machine and a classical music CD played at the same time, and a wave machine and different types of music on the radio. I trained myself to use a variety of music and found that nonvocal music was best. I have also successfully used classic rock, and Spanish music, which has words I do not understand. The only music that absolutely did not work was jazz or rap that had a pounding steady beat. In hotel rooms, I also successfully used music on the radio plus the TV tuned to either the weather channel or movie previews. It had to be something that was totally not interesting. Today, my Ménière's is in remission, so I can now sleep with no added sounds.

Ménière's Is Common

When I go out to dinner with people older than forty and talk about tinnitus, I am discovering that many people have it and it is undiagnosed. They have either tinnitus or dizzy spells. Several of my friends started a low-salt diet and their tinnitus was reduced. That is all they had to do, and it works for many other people too. I had to take a heavy dose of prednisone for a week and then carefully wean off steroids over a six-month period. For several years, my maintenance therapy was a low-salt diet and a low dose of a diuretic water pill called triamterene. If I eat too much salt or forget to take my water pill, I feel a pressure inside my ear and the tinnitus will be worse. Today, I no longer take the water pill. I also had to stop taking estrogen for hot flashes because female hormones make autoimmune problems worse. When I got my ear problems, I had low amounts of B vitamins in my diet due to being gluten-free. Today I take a B-complex supplement.

Autism and autoimmune problems are related. Many of the people with undiagnosed Ménière's, I've discovered, were also parents of children with autism. In many cases, the people had been to their primary doctor, and the doctor did not know what was wrong with them. When I discussed Ménière's with one lady, she said, "That explains why I got dizzy after eating a bag of salty potato chips." Anyone who experiences these symptoms—tinnitus, dizziness, and increasing deafness—should consult a qualified doctor to discuss Ménière's. If the condition is diagnosed, trying one of the suggestions I've mentioned above may help alleviate some of the symptoms.

I picture the frontal cortex as the CEO of a big corporate office tower. Every office in the building is connected to him.

COGNITION AND BRAIN RESEARCH

C ognition is one of my favorite subjects. I'm fascinated by how my thought processes are different from other people's. I love working my mind to figure things out and solve problems, because I am a pure techie nerd. Some people share my fascination, while others are fascinated by the emotional/social parts of thinking and functioning. There are four research centers in the US that have done some of the most important work on how autistic brains differ from normal ones: Dr. Eric Courchesne's group in San Diego; Dr. Nancy Minshew, Dr. Walter Schieder, and their colleagues at the University of Pittsburgh; Dr. Manuel Casanova at the University of Louisville; and the University of Utah group. In my two books, *The Autistic Brain: Helping Different Kinds of Minds to Succeed* and *Visual Thinking: The Hidden Gifts of People Who Think in Pictures, Patterns, and Abstractions*, I cover cognition and brain research.

To briefly summarize, there are three kinds of thinkers. The first type are object visualizers like me who think in pictures. My kind of mind is good at building things, skilled trades, art, working with animals, and photography. Algebra is extremely difficult because there is no way to convert it to pictures. The second type is the visual-spatial thinker, who thinks in patterns. These people are usually good at mathematics and music. The third type is the verbal word thinker, whose thoughts consist of words. Many people are mixtures of the different kinds of thinking. Word thinkers often think in broad concepts, and the two other kinds of thinkers pay attention to details.

There is no black-and-white dividing line between a normal brain and the brains of people on the milder end of the autism spectrum. Autism is a true continuum trait. The mildest forms could be just a personality variation. All brains are comprised of gray matter, analogous to integrated circuits that process information, and white matter that connects the processor units together.

Half the brain by weight is composed of white matter "computer cables" that connect different regions of the brain together. In the normal human brain, every region of the brain has cables that converge on the frontal cortex. This allows the seamless merging of emotions with information stored in different regions. Dr. Minshew explains that in autism, the "cables" that connect feelings to information may be either absent or underdeveloped.

Visualization of Brain Organization

For me to conceptualize how the brain works, I have to use photo-realistic images. Unless I have a photo-realistic picture, it is impossible for me to think. After reading copious numbers of brilliant research papers, I have summarized them by making a pictorial image of brain function. I picture the frontal cortex as the CEO of a big corporate office tower. Every office in the building is connected to him. Brains are highly variable. They can range from one with a highly connected CEO who oversees everything that goes on in the building, to a CEO with weak connections who lets the different departments do what they want. To put it in computer network terms, the brain is a massively interconnected system.

Researchers refer to disorders in the frontal cortex as "executive function" problems, impairing an individual's ability to process and organize information, create plans and sequences, be flexible in their execution, self-regulate responses, and achieve goals. Two major factors determine how the brain network will function. They are the long-distance white matter "cables" that interconnect the different brain departments and smaller local cables that interconnect within a department or between nearby departments. Both Nancy Minshew and Eric Courchesne have done numerous brain scan studies that support this model. In autism, there are fewer long-distance white matter connections and more local connections. More recent literature in 2021 continues to support this model. There is under-connectivity in the language part of the brain. The different brain departments are less interconnected than in a normal brain. As autism gets more severe, the long-distance connections between departments become poorer.

Dr. Manuel Casanova's work has shown that the gray matter processor circuits are also affected. The brain's basic processor circuit is called a *minicolumn*. In people with autism, the minicolumns are smaller. Dr. Casanova did some interesting research that showed that the brains of three deceased scientists also had smaller minicolumns, similar to a brain from a person with autism. A brain with small minicolumns has more processors per square inch, and it will be more efficient at processing detailed information.

Cognitive versus Social Brain

Small minicolumns are connected to white matter cables that wire up local, interoffice communication. Larger minicolumns are connected to big, white matter cables that can connect to far-flung offices on different floors of the building. A brain can be wired to either excel at social interactions with high-speed connections to the emotion centers, the CEO, and the heads of departments, or it can be wired to favor the techies in the math or graphics department. In the brain-favoring local connections, there would be massive cables draped over the tops of a small group of cubicles to wire together computers that are stacked to the ceiling. This would provide the techies with the computers they need to create really cool graphics or foster mathematical savant skills.

Thus, one type of brain network is wired to handle high-speed social information but is lacking detail, and the other is wired to concentrate specifically on the details. We need detail-oriented people in this world; otherwise, there would be no electricity, cars, computers, or even some beautiful works of music. Detail-oriented engineers make sure the lights stay on and the bridges do not fall down.

People on the spectrum tend to have uneven skills. The local departments in the office building are not wired up evenly because there is a shortage of good computer cables. One department gets wired really well to create ability in art, and another department just gets a single weak Wi-Fi connection. I am a pure techie, and having a good career gives my life meaning. I've learned to make the most of the way my brain is hardwired, and I don't feel remorse over missing cables in the social parts of my brain. There are other people on the spectrum who have a few more emotional circuits connected than I do, and they may get frustrated and depressed over their poor ability to relate at a social level. Everyone in life has a different set of strengths and challenges within a unique personality. Using a popular analogy, some people see the glass half empty and are pessimists; others see the glass half full and are optimists. It's no different among people with autism. We still share common personality traits aside from the different ways our brains are wired. Not all the "problems" within autism arise from the autism. Some arise just because of who we are and the personality we each have. Michelle Dawson, a woman with autism, has teamed up with Dr. Laurent Mottron at the University of Montreal to produce research results that clearly show the intelligence of people with autism has been underestimated. Normal children tested with WISC (or Wechsler Intelligence Scale for Children) and Raven's Progressive Matrices will get similar scores on both tests. Autistic children given both tests will get much higher scores on the Raven's, an average of thirty percentile points higher. Raven's tests the ability to see differences and similarities in a series of abstract patterns.

Nonverbal Autism

Both nonverbal and fully verbal individuals with very severe sensory perceptual problems report similar experiences: perception is fragmented, or they may see colors with no clear shapes. Sometimes they report that images break up into pieces like a mosaic. In the visual system, there are separate circuits for color, shape, and motion that must work together to form images. It is likely that in very severe autism, even some of the local circuits are not fully connected. Problems in the white matter circuits that interconnect the thinking and movement parts of the brain may explain why some individuals with autism describe themselves as having a "thinking" self and an "acting" self that can't always coordinate.

Dr. Nancy Minshew and her colleagues state that in severe autism, there is a huge lack of functional connections between the primary sensory cortex and the association areas. To use my office-building analogy, low-level employees can receive information from outside the building on phones or computers, but they are either not connected or too poorly connected to relay that information to many different departments. Teachers and caregivers of individuals with very severe autism often report that the person has some areas of real intelligence, even though they are constantly flapping. These brains may be like an entire office building where most of the interdepartmental and outside network connections are not functioning, but off in one corner are a few cubicles of normal employees with one static-filled, unreliable mobile phone line to the outside world.

Over the years, I have observed that people on the more severe end of the spectrum are often more "normal" in their emotional/social processing. This can be seen in the writings of Tito Mukhopadhyay (*Understanding Nonverbal Autism*) and others who can type independently and describe their inner world. To return to the office-building analogy, there are a few employees in the more emotional and social parts of the office building—the human service and sales departments—that still have phone lines intact and functioning. However, everything in the techie department is broken.

This idea of interconnectivity problems among the different brain departments explains why the autism spectrum is so variable and why no two individuals are the same in their functioning and understanding. It all depends on where the good computer cables hook up. Dr. Courchesne's work shows that there is an early abnormal overgrowth of white matter in autism. As the severity of autism increases, the white matter overgrowth increases. This may leave fewer good computer cables to form long-distance connections between departments, and those connections are necessary for the office as a whole to function efficiently and collect information from all sources.

Is Autism the Price for a Human Brain?

The genetic mechanisms that cause humans to have a large brain may be the same genes that cause autism and other disorders. Researchers J. M. Sikela at the Colorado School of Medicine and V. B. Searles at the University of California have found that a copy number variation in the chromosome locus 1q21 may cause both autism and schizophrenia. Copy numbers of genetic code are like volume controls for different traits. A particular piece of genetic code may be either duplicated many times or have copies deleted. Extra copies may cause autism and a larger head, and too few copies may cause schizophrenia. Just the right number of copies will create a so-called "normal" human brain.

For years, I have maintained that a person's brain can be either more cognitive (thinking) or more social-emotional. A certain amount of variation in copy number would probably be part of normal human personality variation. Too much variation in copy number (adding too many extra copies or deleting too many copies) may cause an obvious abnormality such as speech delay or hallucinations.

Autism and schizophrenia are brain development opposites. Autism may cause the brain to develop extra processing power in the back of the brain for memory, math, art, or music; a brain with schizophrenia may not develop enough connections. This might explain why schizophrenic symptoms develop in late adolescence. At this time, a process called synaptic pruning trims and fine-tunes neural connections. Since the network is skimpy, normal *synaptic pruning* may cause the network to start failing. When the network loses too many connections, symptoms such as hallucinations and delusions may start.

Human Brain Development Is Unstable

The genetic systems that have created the human brain may lack stability. The genetic 1q21.1 locus contains a gene called NOTCH2NL. To create a large human brain, it allows undifferentiated stem cells to greatly multiply. This provides more cells that can turn into brain cells. Dr. I. T. Fidder and his associates state, "NOTCH2NL genes may have contributed to the rapid evolution of the larger human neocortex, accompanied by loss of genomic stability of the 1q21.1 locus and resulting in recurrent neurodevelopmental disorders."

Further Evidence of Autistic Traits Is Part of Normal Personality Variation

In the animal kingdom, there are animals that are social and animals that are more solitary. Lions, for example, are more social mammals than tigers, leopards, polar bears, and chipmunks. Dr. Jared Reser at the University of California conducted an extensive literature review and found that solitary mammals share many of the characteristics found in autism. Solitary mammals have less oxytocin (social hormones) than those who live in social groups, causing an increased stress response during social encounters. They also have a reduced reaction to social separation from herd-mates. In other words, they have a greater tolerance for being alone. Autism, in its milder forms, is simply normal personality variation.

Reading these papers was an eye-opening experience. First of all, they indicate that the genetics of autism are also the genetics of normal brain variation in both human and animal social behavior. Secondly, the genetic mechanisms that cause autism are the same genetic mechanisms that gave humans a greatly expanded brain.

Additional Reading

Casanova, M.E., A.E. Switala, J. Tripp, and M. Fitzgerald. 2007. Comparative Minicolumnar Morphometry of Three Distinguished Scientists. Autism National Autistic Society, UK, *Autism*, 11(6):557-569.

Casanova, M.E. et al. 2006. Minicolumnar abnormalities in autism. *Acta Neuropathologica* 112: 187-303.

Davis, J.M. et al. (2019) A third linear association between Olduvai (DUF1220) copy number and severity of the classic symptoms of inherited autism, *American Journal of Psychiatry*, 8.

Fiddes, I.T. et al. (2018) Human-specific NOTCH2NL genes affect notch signaling and cortical neurogenesis, *Cell* 31:1356-1369.

Pennisi, E. (2018) New copies of old gene drove brain expansion, *Science*, 360:951.

Reser, J.E. (2014) Solitary mammals provide an animal model for autism spectrum disorders, *Journal of Comparative Psychology*, 128(1):99-113.

Sikela, J.M. (2018) Genomic tradeoffs: Are autism and schizophrenia a steep price for the human brain, *Human Genetics*, 137(1):1-13.

Courchesne, E., and K. Pierce. 2005. Brain overgrowth in autism during a critical time in development: Implications for frontal pyramidal neuron and interneuron development and connectivity. *International Journal of Developmental Neuroscience* 23: 153-170.

Davis, J.M. et al. 2019. A third linear association between Olduvai (DUF1220) copy number and severity of the classic symptoms of inherited autism, *American Journal of Psychiatry*, 8.

Dawson, M., I. Soulieres, M.A. Gernsbacher, and L. Mottron. 2007. The level and nature of autistic intelligences. *Psychological Science* 18: 657- 662.

Fiddes, I.T. et al. (2018) Human specific NOTCH2NL genes affect notch signaling and cortical neurogenesis, *Cell* 31:1356-1369.

Hughes, J. 2007. Autism: The first firm finding underconnectivity? *Epilepsy and Behavior* 11(1): 20-24.

Miller, B.L. et al. 1998. Emergence of art talent in frontal temporal dementia. *Neurology* 51: 978-981.

Min, L. et al. (2022) Atypical structural connectivity of language networks in autism spectrum disorder: A meta-analysis of diffusion tenses imaging studies, *Autism Research* 15(9):1585-1602.

Minshew, N.J. and D.L. Williams. 2007. The new neurology of autism. *Archives of Neurology* 64: 945-950.

Maximo, J.O., et.al. 2014. The implications of brain connectivity in the neuropsychology of autism. *Neuropsychology Review* 24:16-31.

Pennisi, E. 2018. New copies if old gene drove brain expansion, *Science*, 360:951.

Reser, J.E. (2014) Solitary mammals provide an animal model for autism spectrum disorders, *Journal of Comparative Psychology*, 128(1):99-113.

Sikela, J.M. (2018) Genomic tradeoffs: Are autism and schizophrenia a steep price for the human brain, *Human Genetics*, 137(1):1-13.

Silk, T.J. et al. 2006. Visuospatial processing and the function of prefrontal-parietal networks in autism spectrum disorders: A functional MRI study. *American Journal of Psychiatry* 163: 14401443

Tarai, L. et al. (2021) The directionality of frontal posterior brain connectivity is associated with the degree of individual autistic traits, *Brain Science*.

Wan, J. et al (2000) Increased EEG coherence in long distance and short distance connectivity in children with autism spectrum disorder, *Brain and Behavior*.

Wicker, I. 2005. Autistic brains out of sync. *Science* 308: 18561858.

CHAPTER THREE

UNDERSTANDING
NONVERBAL
AUTISM

These individuals are highly aware of their surroundings and have self-learned far more than parents and teachers imagine. It's their bodies that don't work, not their minds.

To understand the mind of a child or adult who is completely nonverbal, without oral, signed, written, or typed language, you must leave the world of thinking in words. This can be quite challenging for many people. Our society functions through the spoken word. For the majority of people, words are their "native language." It is difficult for them to step outside this very basic way of relating and imagine something else. Some neurotypical people, especially those with stronger creative sides, can do this. Other neurotypical people struggle immensely in understanding this concept.

I think in pictures. It's been that way forever for me. When I was very young, before any speech or language training, there were no words in my head. Now, words narrate the pictures in my imagination, but pictures remain my primary "language."

For a minute, try to imagine an inner world of picture-based or sensory-based thoughts. The closest analogy that may make sense to most neurotypical people who think in words is to recall a recent dream. Many dreams do not contain language. They are flowing sequences of pictures, with associated emotional impressions. Sometimes these pictorial narrations make sense and we come away with a "message" from the dream.

Many times, however, the images are strange and disconnected from one another, and we awake scratching our heads and wondering, "What was that dream all about?" If the nonverbal person has a severe visual processing problem, now imagine that your visual system is providing jumbled images, like a pixelated video screen with a poor satellite signal. All the common sounds that most people ignore, such as the sound of people walking or doors opening and closing, cannot be filtered out. This is what a nonverbal person may face. Hearing individual conversations may be difficult and may be like struggling with a mobile phone with a weak signal.

To imagine a nonverbal person's world, I shut my eyes and think with each of my individual senses. What would thinking in touch be like if I could not rely on the distorted input from my dysfunctional visual and auditory systems? How might I function if I could only relate to my world through my sense of smell? As an exercise in touch and smell thought, the reader could think about a vacation on the beach. There are usually vivid impressions of the color and sound of the ocean, the feel of the warm sand, and the salty smell. When a nonverbal person thinks or daydreams, maybe there are no words going through his head.

There are only sensory impressions, such as images, sounds, smells, tactile impressions, and taste sensations coming into his consciousness. If the person has severe problems with both visual and auditory processing, his brain may rely on his other senses to make sense of his world. His only coherent thoughts may be in touch, taste, or smell sensations. These forms of sensory input may be the only way he obtains accurate information about his environment. Maybe this is why some nonverbal individuals touch, tap, and smell things. It's how they learn about their world. Our typical way of life, and especially our education system, is largely based on visual and auditory sharing of information.

Imagine how difficult mere existence would be if those information channels were constantly turned off or functioned poorly in an individual. Parents, teachers, and therapists need to be good detectives in working with nonverbal individuals to figure out which senses are working best. For some, the auditory sense is preferred, and for others, it's vision. For a minority of people, the sense of touch may be the primary learning channel. A basic principle is to use the sensory system that works the best. However, this will be highly variable among different nonverbal individuals.

Nonverbal, with or without Cognitive Impairment

The reader may wonder where I concocted all these ideas about nonverbal people's perceptions. They are based on neuroscience knowledge, coupled with reports from many verbal individuals who can describe their very severe sensory problems. Many individuals who have more severe sensory problems than mine describe sensory scrambling or the shutdown of one or more senses. This occurs more frequently when the individuals are tired or in a highly stimulating environment, such as a large supermarket. Included in this section are three articles about Tito and Carly. They are nonverbal individuals who can type independently and, in striking detail, describe their inner world. Tito has written about disordered, jumbled visual perceptions.

He also described a thinking self that exists separate from an acting self. He cannot control some of his flapping movements. His mind and body are not integrated. The human brain contains circuits for color, shape, and motion. These circuits have to work together to form images. Tito describes visual perception where it is obvious that these circuits are not working together. He may see the color of an object before he can identify it by shape. For parents and teachers who work with nonverbal individuals, I strongly recommend Tito's book, *How Can I Talk If My Lips Don't Move?* Two other books that will provide great insight into the world of nonverbal people with autism are *The Reason I Jump*, by Noaki Higashida, and *Carly's Voice*. I recommend these books because all three of their authors can use a keyboard without anyone having to touch them. If somebody is holding the child's arm or wrist, they may be the author of the child's writing instead of the child.

As a society, we equate intelligence with language. Smart people are verbal people. The verbal people who can express themselves best are assumed to be the most intelligent. People who can't use language well are perceived as dumb. We don't usually stop and question whether oral-motor skills, rather than intelligence, might be causing the language impairment. No, we do just the opposite and almost instantaneously judge the nonverbal person as being mentally impaired. *Poor guy—he can't talk.* And, in our minds, we continue with the most damaging thought of all: *He must not have anything to say.*

This is very true within the autism community. We assume that those who are nonverbal, especially children who have been nonverbal since birth, have reduced or limited cognitive abilities. Many professionals believe that 75 percent of these individuals function at an intellectually disabled level, based on IQ scores. This sets up a vicious cycle: We expect less from these kids, so they receive fewer opportunities to learn. We don't challenge them to learn because we've already decided that they can't. We test these children for IQ, using testing instruments that are largely ill-suited to this population, and then point to their low scores as confirmation of impaired mental functioning.

The way I see it, it's time we rethink nonverbal individuals with autism and realize that the preconceived notions we've been using to relate to and educate this population over the past twenty years are flat-out wrong. Luckily, other professionals in the autism community are coming to the same conclusion, and research is shedding light on the hidden abilities within this population. Professionals have generally agreed that about 50 percent of individuals with autism will never speak. Catherine Lord, a University of Michigan pioneer in autism research, suggests we may be way off the mark. In her 2004 study sample of children who received a diagnosis and began undergoing treatment at age two, only 14 percent remained nonverbal by age nine, and 35 to 45 percent could speak fluently.

Our current perceptions about nonverbal individuals with autism are also being stretched by people on the spectrum, like Tito, Carly Fleischman, Naoki Higashida, and others, who are coming forth and writing about their rich inner worlds and abilities. Bit by bit, they are deflating the notion that not being able to speak means not having anything to say. Through the increased use of augmentative and alternative communication aids with nonverbal individuals, we are discovering that many children with autism have taught themselves to read. These individuals are highly aware of their surroundings and have self-learned far more than parents and teachers imagine. It's their bodies that don't work, not their minds.

Carly Fleischman describes having great difficulty with filtering out environmental sensory input. She is a normal teenage girl locked in a body she has difficulty controlling. Naoki Higashida describes being embarrassed by uncontrollable movements. Both Tito and Carly have to exert great effort to block out extraneous stimuli and pay attention. When I visited Tito, he could answer only three questions before he needed to rest. iPads and other tablet computers have helped many nonverbal individuals. Typing is easier for them on a table, because the typed letter on the virtual keyboard appears right next to the keyboard. The individual does not need to shift his gaze to see the letter. Shifting his gaze between the keyboard and a desktop or laptop screen is very difficult.

And, these individuals have a lot to say. Amanda Baggs is one such woman, and her nine-minute YouTube clip, "In My Language," is illuminating to all who watch it. As it opens, we see her rocking back and forth, flapping her hands in front of a large window. She goes through a series of odd repetitive behaviors, all the while accompanied by an almost eerie hum. She swats at a necklace with her hand, slaps a sheet of paper against a window, runs her hand over a computer keyboard, and flicks a metal band against a doorknob. Then the words "A Translation" appear on the screen, and the twenty-seven-year-old nonverbal autistic woman mesmerizes us with a highly articulate explanation of her thoughts and actions. She explains how touch, taste, and smell provide her with a "constant conversation" with her environment. She challenges our neurotypical way of thinking about nonverbal individuals in a manner that cannot be ignored. And I, for one, applaud her and others who are speaking out about what it means, and doesn't mean, to be nonverbal and have autism. It's about time.

In our interactions with nonverbal individuals with autism, it is critical that we accurately determine their level of ability and challenge and not automatically make assumptions based on their verbal language capabilities or their IQ scores. It is true that many highly impaired individuals with autism exist who also have accompanying intellectual disability. But, that percentage may be far less than what we currently assume. When a person who is nonverbal acquires the ability to use language, it changes his life. Tito told me that before he could type, he had "emptiness." It appears that in some cases, nonverbal autism is a "locked-in syndrome," where a normal mind is trapped in a sensory and motor system that does not work. I hypothesize that nonverbal autism is very different than fully verbal autism. Fully verbal autism may be more of a lack of social-emotional relatedness, and nonverbal individuals may have more normal emotional systems locked in by faulty sensory systems. There is further information on sensory oversensitivity in chapter 3 and in my book *The Autistic Brain*.

Slow Processing of Information

For most nonverbal and impaired individuals with autism, the brain processes information very slowly. They may have fewer input channels open to receive information, or their connections may work like a dial-up rather than a high-speed Internet connection. They need much more time to switch gears between different tasks. In autism and many other developmental disorders, attention shifting is slow, and nonverbal impaired individuals are often slower than individuals with milder forms of autism. In her lectures, Lorna King, one of the early pioneers in using sensory integration, warned all therapists attending her meetings about a phenomenon called "clipping." Clipping can occur in individuals who are both verbal and nonverbal. Attention shifting can be so slow that the person may miss half the information the teacher is trying to convey to them. This is most likely to happen when the child's attention has to be shifted to a new task. For example, if I said to a child playing with his toy, "The juice is on the table," the child may hear only "on the table." To avoid this problem, the parent or teacher should first capture the child's attention with a phrase like, "Tommy, I need to tell you something," and then deliver the instruction or important information. If half of that first phrase is "clipped," it does not matter, because now the input channel is open and the statement about the juice can get through.

Fear Is the Main Emotion

All behavior occurs for a reason. When a nonverbal impaired person has a tantrum, fear may be the main motivator. There is now functional magnetic resonance imaging evidence that sensory oversensitivity is associated with increased activation of the amygdala (the fear center in the brain). In my own case, small, high-pitched noises that occur at night still set off a little twinge of fear in me. The big, heart-pounding, fearful reactions I used to have during my twenties are now controlled with antidepressant drugs. Trying to eliminate these big-fear reactions through cognitive or behavioral methods didn't work for me. Self-reports from other individuals also indicate that certain sounds or sensations cause panic attacks. Recently, brain imaging at the University of Utah showed that the amygdala in my brain is enlarged. This may explain my increased fear responses. If an individual is nonverbal and his receptive learning is impaired, harmless things such as a certain room or a particular person may be associated with a stimulus that hurts, such as a smoke alarm. In some cases, the individual might associate the dreadful sound with something he was looking at when the alarm went off. If he was looking at a teacher's blue jacket, he may develop a blue-jacket fear. I know this sounds odd, but these associative fear memories occur all the time in animals. A dog often fears the place where he got hit by a car instead of being afraid of cars. If these associations can be figured out, it may be possible to remove the feared object. I discuss fear memories in more depth in my book *Animals in Translation*.

A person with severe autism can easily panic if something new is suddenly introduced. A surprise birthday party can trigger a tantrum instead of pleasure. It is best to gradually habituate the child to the things he or she will experience at the party. This is very similar to habituating horses to tolerate the new, scary things they will see at a horse show. They need to gradually get used to new things such as flags and balloons at home, before they go to a show. Individuals with severe autism can learn to like new things. The best way to introduce them is to let the child or adult gradually approach and explore them at his or her own pace and inclination. Some nonverbal individuals may explore them by touching, smelling, or tasting. They need to be provided with a specific place where they are allowed to do this kind of exploration, because licking things at the grocery store is not appropriate behavior. Nonverbal impaired people are usually able to learn that certain activities are only allowed in certain places. For instance, if the person does not want to taste a new food, he or she may need to explore it first by touching or smelling it. This activity should be done away from the dining room because touching and smearing food is not appropriate behavior in the dining room.

Self-Injurious Behavior (SIB)

Some nonverbal individuals, and even some highly verbal individuals, engage in banging their heads or biting themselves. Reports from people on the spectrum have revealed that many of these problems stem from severe sensory issues. In this case, the child may be hyposensitive—lacking in sensory input—rather than the more typical hypersensitivity (too much input) that is often the case within the autism population. In some of these cases, individuals do not realize they are being self-injurious, because they have tactile or body boundary issues. For example, when they are tired or upset, they cannot determine where their foot ends and the floor begins. They may not feel themselves sitting on a chair at school, so they squirm or bounce in the chair to induce the sensory input they need to feel stable.

Lorna King found that a child who self-abuses often feels no pain. Children may dig at their skin to the point of drawing blood because their sensory receptors return no tactile sensation, as would happen in a typical person. After King introduced children to activities that provided calming sensory stimulation, such as deep pressure or slow swinging, pain sensation returned. She has seen children who used to bang their heads start to hit their heads and stop before they did so, because they know it will hurt now. You may also want to try the environmental enrichment method of pairing different odors with different textures for the child to touch. See the chapter on environmental enrichment for more information. For some severe cases of SIB, treatment with the opiate-blocking drug naltrexone may be helpful. There is an excellent open-access article by Dr. Sandman and Dr. Kemp from the University of California in the Additional Reading list.

The best approach for controlling SIB is an integrated approach. A combination of behavioral analysis, sensory therapy, conventional medications, and biomedical interventions, such as diets and supplements, often works best. The big mistake that many people make when treating SIB is to get too single-minded in their approach. Some people try to use just behavioral analysis and never use a drug. Others use drugs and nothing else. Both single-minded approaches are wrong. A drug-only approach leads to a case of a sleepy "drug zombie," and a behavioral-only approach without any intervention to reduce nervous system arousal may lead to the use of bad procedures, such as long periods of restraint.

Does the Nonverbal Person Understand Speech?

In some cases, nonverbal people have receptive language and can understand what is being said. In other cases, they do not. Nonverbal people are masters at reading slight differences in a teacher's or parent's actions. I had one parent tell me that her child has ESP, because he is already waiting at the door before his mother even gets her car keys or purse. It is likely that the individual is sensing slight differences in behavior before it's time to get the keys or purse. There may be some hustle and bustle activities, such as throwing out the newspaper. If the child has severe visual processing problems, he may be responding to the sounds of the paper being crushed in the trashcan.

In some situations, the nonverbal individual may be responding to a gesture rather than a word. If you point to the juice or turn your head toward it, the person may perceive your actions. One way to test receptive language is to ask the person to do something odd. An example would be to ask the child to put his or her book on the chair. In some nonverbal individuals, verbal language is impossible, but they learn to read and express themselves through typing. Their speech circuits are scrambled, but they can still communicate through the typed word.

Typing Independently

Some non-speaking individuals can learn how to type independently. Teaching how to type independently should definitely be considered, if a child does not learn speech after five or six years of age. There are also some speaking individuals who can express their thoughts more clearly by typing. Learning to type will be much easier for the individual if they are able to see both the letter key they pushed and appearance of the letter on the screen without shifting their gaze. Tablets are recommended because the letters appear right next to the top of the virtual keyboard. Both laptops and desktops force the individual to shift their gaze from the keyboard to the top of the screen. This is difficult for many autistic people. One innovative teacher put a portable keyboard on a box to raise it up to the top of the screen. When the person typed, the print appeared next to the keyboard.

The goal is to achieve the ability to type independently with no one touching either the person or the device. This is true independent typing. There is always the question of cues that could change the content of the text. In the beginning, a wrist support may be needed. Eventually this support should be phased out and removed. The tablet, or cardboard printed keyboard, should not be held by a person. This may provide opportunities for cues from the teacher.

There are non-speaking autistic people who have good minds trapped in a dysfunctional body. We need to help free their minds. When I asked Tito what it was like before typing, he said EMPTINESS. Typing can open the door to many opportunities.

Additional Reading

Fleischman, A., Fleischman, C. 2012. *Carly's Voice: Breaking Through Autism*. New York, NY: Touchstone Books.

Fouse, B., Wheeler, M. 1997. *A Treasure Chest of Behavioral Strategies for Individuals with Autism*. Arlington, TX: Future Horizons.

Grandin, T., Johnson, C. 2005. *Animals in Translation*. New York, NY: Scribner.

Grandin, T., Panek, R. 2013. *The Autistic Brain*. New York, NY: Houghton Mifflin Harcourt.

Higashida, N. and Mitchell, D. (2017) *Fall Down 7 Times, Get Up 8: A Young Man's Voice from the Silence of Autism*, Random House, New York.

Horvath, K., Perman, J.A. 2002. "Autism and Gastrointestinal Symptoms." *Current Gastroenterology Reports* 4:251-258.

Kern, J.K., et al. 2007. "Sensory Correlations in Autism." *Autism* 11:123-134.

Mukhopadhyay, T.J. (2011) *How Can I Talk if My Lips Don't Move?* Available as Amazon Kindle and audiobook.

Sandman, C.A., Kemp, A.S. 2011. "Opioid Antagonists May Reverse Endogenous Opiate Dependence in Treatment of Self Injurious Behavior." *Pharmaceuticals* 4:366-381.

Savarese, R.J. 2007. *Reasonable People: A Memoir of Autism and Adoption—On the Meaning of Family and the Politics of Neurological Difference*. New York, NY: Other Press. (This book describes successful teaching strategies for teaching nonverbal people to type.)

Schaller, S. 1995. *A Man without Words*. Berkeley, CA: University of California Press.

Schumann, C.M., et al. 2009. "Amygdala Enlargement in Toddlers with Autism Related to Severity of Social and Communication Impairments." *Biological Psychiatry* 66:942-943.

Williams, D. 1996. *Autism: An Inside-Out Approach*. London, England: Jessica Kingsley Publishers.

Wolfgang, A., Pierce, L., Teder-Salejarvi, W. A., Courchesne, E., Hillyard, S.A. 2005. "Auditory Spatial Localization and Attention Deficits in Autistic Adults." *Cognitive Brain Research* 23:221-234.

Wolman, D. 2008. "The Truth about Autism: Scientists Reconsider What They Think They Know." *Wired Magazine*, 16:03.

A SOCIAL TEENAGER TRAPPED INSIDE

Some individuals with autism who appear to be intellectually disabled have a good mind trapped inside a dysfunctional body that they cannot control. Carly Fleischmann appeared to have no skills at all when she was a child. She had no speech, and she was either in constant motion, destroying things, or sitting alone rocking. The only thing she seemed to care about was potato chips. When she was given a device that had pictures that spoke words when pressed, she quickly learned how to use it. But she found it difficult to press the button for a really needed bathroom break when the button for potato chips was so enticing.

Teachers sometimes underestimate a child's abilities. One teacher was going to delete the keyboard function on Carly's communication device. If this had happened, Carly's parents would have never learned that she knew words. One day Carly typed, "Help teeth hurt." After this happened, a program was started to teach her more words. Every object in the house was labeled. It turned out that Carly was taking in lots of information even though she appeared to not be paying attention.

As Carly slowly became literate, she explained how typing required great effort. She was extremely anxious, and often she would type only with people she knew. Today Carly is typing independently, and she attends a gifted program at her local public high school. She explains how it was so difficult to control her body and sit still. Unlike me, Carly was interested in boys, movie stars, and all the things that a typical teenage girl would be infatuated with. When she was on national TV, she knew she would have to remain still and have no outbursts. She said it would be easier if the cameraman was really cute. To Carly, autism does not define who she is. She wishes her brain and body could be fixed so that normal activities would be easier.

Sensory Bombardment

Carly thinks in pictures that rush at her all at once. I can control the images that come into my mind, but Carly cannot. Filtering out background stimulation is difficult for Carly, and she often has a hard time understanding what other people are saying.

Carly eloquently describes how sensory stimuli intrude and make listening to a conversation difficult. Carly reports that she often hears only one or two words in each sentence. She describes how cascades of many different stimuli block out the conversation. For example, when she is in a quiet coffee shop talking to another person, the relatively low background noise and visual stimuli of the coffee shop can be filtered out. She calls this "audio filtering," which is often very difficult. Her ability to audio filter becomes overloaded when, for example, a person passes by her table with strong perfume. Now, the previously blocked-out sounds of the coffee maker and the sight of a door opening and closing all rush in and block out the conversation.

Carly is able to audio filter when the background stimulation is low, but when her audio filtering is overloaded, stimuli from all her senses cascade into her brain and turn everything into chaos. At this point, controlling a meltdown is almost impossible.

To help control meltdowns and body movements, Carly does have to take medication. Controlling herself requires both intense willpower and medication. When she was young, potato chips were the motivation. Today, being able to participate in typical girl interests is the motivator to control her body.

What Is Autism?

Carly's story makes one think, what is autism? In my case, autism is part of who I am, and I do not have the social interests that Carly has. I have no desire to change my brain or be cured. At the so-called high end of the spectrum, autism may be a disorder of the social circuits in the brain. At the other end of the spectrum, it may be a "locked-in" disorder where a social person is trapped inside a dysfunctional body and sensory system.

I need to warn the reader to be realistic. Not every child on the more severe end of the spectrum can be Carly, but teachers and parents who are observant can see glimpses of true intelligence in individuals who are unable to "speak."

Additional Reading

Fleischmann, A., and C. Fleischmann. 2012. *Carly's Voice*. New York: Touchstone.

The more we learn about the inner mind of individuals with severe autism, the better able we become to accurately gauge their many abilities and help them achieve their hidden potential.

UNDERSTANDING THE MIND OF A NONVERBAL PERSON WITH AUTISM

While huge advances have been made over the last few years in understanding "higher functioning" individuals with autism/Asperger's, we still know quite little about the world of the more severely affected individual with autism. In 2007, Tito Mukhopadhyay wrote a book titled *The Mind Tree* that opened to the world the mind of a nonverbal boy with severe autism. Tito's new book, *How Can I Talk If My Lips Don't Move?* is equally compelling and highly informative, and should be required reading for everybody who works with nonverbal individuals with autism.

Presumed Intelligence

Tito's mother, Soma, was a brilliant teacher. She invented all kinds of innovative ways to teach her nonverbal, profoundly autistic son to write and type without assistance. Right from the beginning, Soma assumed Tito was not stupid, so she exposed her young child to many interesting things. She also read to him constantly. She read him children's books and adult books such as Plato, Keats, history, and geometry. When she played with him on a swing, she explained the physics of a pendulum. She also took him to many interesting places, such as the outdoor food market, other people's houses, and the train station. Even though Tito had all the characteristics of a person with low-functioning autism, he was absorbing large amounts of knowledge. Soma instinctively knew that she needed to fill his brain with information.

Sensory Jumble and Panic

Tito's sensory world was a jumble of colors, sounds, and smells. Hearing was his dominant sense, and his mother's voice reading to him became a familiar sound that provided order in the chaos. Any little changes in his routine caused panic and a temper tantrum. Tito describes flicking the lights on and off because it brought order to the overwhelming, scattered jumble of sensory overload. Tito is mono-channel, and he can only attend to one sense at a time. Seeing and hearing at the same time is impossible, and his best learning occurs in the morning before he gets tired.

Anything new was totally frightening because the feeling, sight, or sound of a new object was so intense it caused sensory overload and panic. Soma slowly introduced new things, and Tito gradually learned to tolerate them. When he got overwhelmed, Tito explained how flapping calmed him down and made him happy. However, had he been allowed to do it all day, he never would have learned anything. Small amounts of this type of stimming were allowed so he could calm down.

Tito Hates Unfinished Tasks and Things

Soma figured out how to motivate the completion of a task by doing part of it and then leaving a part unfinished to motivate Tito to finish it. She used a hand-over-hand technique to teach skills such as putting on a shirt, putting on shoes, and holding a pencil. Touch provided Tito with more reliable information than vision. To teach a task such as putting on a T-shirt, Soma placed her hands over Tito's and "walked" his hands through the entire task. Gradually, she left more and more of the task unfinished so Tito had to finish it. For example, she stopped helping when his arms were through the sleeves and the shirt was halfway over his head. Tito had to pull the shirt the rest of the way himself. This teaching had to be done slowly over several months so Tito's motor memory would learn the entire task.

Difficulty Naming Objects

A psychologist testing Tito could mistakenly think he could not name common objects. He can, but he must do it in a roundabout, associative manner. His mind is totally associative. To retrieve the name of an object, he has to be given time to find the word in his memory by providing the definition of the word. Writing the definition enables his associative way of thinking to find the word. When shown a picture of a flower, he is not able to simply say, "Flower." He has to say, "A soft-petaled part of a plant is a flower." Tito can write this definition because he was exposed to words such as *petal*. Soma constantly showed him interesting things and pointed to the parts and named them.

This wonderful book, *How Can I Talk If My Lips Don't Move?* will provide parents, educators, and everybody who works with nonverbal individuals insights that will help them work more effectively with this population. Dr. Margaret Bauman, neurologist at Massachusetts General Hospital, emphasizes that we wrongly assume that 75 percent of nonverbal individuals are intellectually disabled. The more we learn about the inner mind of individuals with severe autism, the better able we become to accurately gauge their many abilities and help them achieve their hidden potential.

Additional Reading

Mukhopadhyay, Tito Rajarshi. 2008. *How Can I Talk If My Lips Don't Move?* New York: Arcade Publishing.

When I asked him what his life was like before he learned to type, he responded with the word "empty."

TITO LIVES IN A WORLD OF SENSORY SCRAMBLING

I first met Tito Mukhopadhyay* in a quiet medical library. He looked like a typical nonverbal, low-functioning teenager with autism. When he entered the room, he picked up a bright yellow journal and smelled it. He then ran around and flapped.

His mother pulled him over to the computer where I sat and invited me to ask Tito a question about autism. I told her I wanted to ask him about something different, where cueing or prior memorization of an answer would be impossible. From the bottom of a nearby pile of magazines, I found an old *Scientific American*. As I thumbed through the magazine, I found an illustration of an astronaut riding a horse. When I showed Tito the picture, he

---

* At the age of three, Tito Mukhopadhyay was diagnosed with severe autism, but his mother, Soma, refused to accept the conventional wisdom of the time that her son would be unable to interact with the outside world. She read to him, taught him to write in English, and challenged him to write his own stories. The result of their efforts is a remarkable book, *The Mind Tree: A Miraculous Child Breaks the Silence of Autism*, written when Tito was between eight and eleven years old. It comprises a broad collection of profound and startling philosophical writings about growing up under the most challenging of circumstances and how it feels to be locked inside an autistic body and mind. Tito has another book that will provide tremendous insight into how he lives in a world of sensory fragmentation.

Another fantastic story is *The Reason I Jump*. People who work with children and adults who remain nonverbal should read all three books in the Additional Reading list. These three books are all written by nonverbal individuals. They will give you insight into a world of sensory scrambling.

quickly typed, "Apollo II on a horse." This convinced me there was a good brain trapped inside Tito's dysfunctional body.

At a recent conference in Canada, I had another opportunity to talk with Tito. Throughout our conversation, his mother had to keep prompting him to attend to the computer and respond to my questions. I was curious about his sensory systems, so I asked him what his vision was like. He said he saw fragments of color, shapes, and motion. This is a more severe version of the fragmented perception that Donna Williams has described in her books. When I asked him what his life was like before he learned to type, he responded with the word "empty." Despite intervention, Tito still has a very short attention span. He could type only a few short sentences while we were together before he succumbed to sensory overload.

Visual processing challenges such as Tito experiences may stem from abnormal brain connections, according to Dr. Eric Courchesne. The brain has three types of visual perception circuits, each different for color, shape, and motion. In the typical brain, these circuits work together to merge the three visual components into a stable image. Research has shown that in autism, there is a lack of interconnections between different parts of the brain. Dr. Eric Courchesne suggests that in autistic brains, large neurons that integrate different brain systems are abnormal. He states that autism may be an unusual disconnection disorder.

Not all nonverbal children with autism can be like Tito, but he is a prime example of a person with a part of the brain having many broken connections with the outside world. Because of their fragmented abilities, it is important that parents and professionals introduce different modes of communication and social connection, like the keyboard, to children with autism at an early age so that another Tito is not trapped in emptiness.

Additional Reading

Courchesne, E. 2004. "Brain Development in Autism: Early Overgrowth Followed by Premature Arrest of Growth." *Mental Retardation and Developmental Disabilities* 10: 106-111.

Fleishmann, A., and Fleishmann, C. 2012. *Carly's Voice: Breaking Through Autism*. New York, NY: Touchstone Books.

Higashida, N. and Mitchell, D. 2013. *The Reason I Jump: The Inner Voice of a Thirteen-Year-Old Boy with Autism*. New York, NY: Random House.

Mukhopadhyay, T. 2008. *How Can I Talk If My Lips Don't Move?* New York, NY: Arcade Publishing.

CHAPTER FOUR

ADULT ISSUES & EMPLOYMENT

Having an interesting career has given my life purpose and meaning.

When an individual with autism graduates from high school or college, getting employment is often a big problem. Many studies have shown that discouragingly low percentages of individuals on the spectrum remain gainfully employed. To solve this problem, work experiences should start before graduation from high school. In the next section, I will describe my many work experiences, which started at age thirteen.

An evidence-based randomized clinical trial by Paul H. Wehman at Virginia Commonwealth University shows that working for a year before graduating greatly increases employability, from 6.25 percent to 87.5 percent. To be successful, the program requires a willing and cooperative employer, combined with parents, teachers, and state vocational agencies that all work together. Each student in the study participated in a nine-month intensive internship at a large hospital. The individuals learned to do a job that used their ability to pay attention to details. Examples of the jobs were setting up surgical instruments for complex procedures or cleaning specialized equipment. Sometimes, more time was required to learn the job, but when the task was mastered, performance was excellent. Students who are slow to learn need to be given an opportunity to develop their skills.

The name of the program is Project SEARCH, and the students are now working in jobs at 24 percent above minimum wage. Project SEARCH now branches out into non-hospital work, and their approach is very effective. Another effective program is TACT in Denver that trains young autistic adults to become CAT mechanics. It has three phases. The first phase is the exploration phase, where the autistic individuals can try different trades. The second phase is small mechanics classes with both a mechanic and a job coach. Here, the student is taught both job and life skills. After the mechanics training, in the third phase, the person is moved into a job as a mechanic for a car dealership. They will have a job coach at the workplace for several months. TACT has contracts with car companies to put mechanics in car dealerships. The success rate is about 80 percent.

It is really important for an individual on the autism spectrum to have a boss that understands them. I have observed that changing bosses is risky. When I worked as livestock editor of the *Arizona Farmer* in the early 1970s, I was almost fired when the magazine was sold and I got a new boss. He thought I was weird. I was able to save my job by showing him a portfolio of all my articles. He was impressed by my work. Unfortunately, I have observed talented autistic individuals being either fired or laid off when the boss changed. Valerie Marin and her colleagues at the University of Montreal did a study that showed that the quality of the relationship with the boss was important for continued employment.

There are certain types of jobs that people with autism would be really good at. Laurent Mottron at the University of Montreal explains that people on the spectrum excel at work that involves analyzing large research data sets and paying attention to details. She emphasizes how to capitalize on the unique abilities of people on the autism spectrum. The way I see it, many of the challenges within this population arise from the less rigid style of child-rearing that is prevalent today. During the 1950s, *all* children were taught manners and social rules and "behaving." Mothers made sure their children learned to say "please" and "thank you," knew how to play with other kids, and understood appropriate and inappropriate behavior. There were hard and fast rules to behavior back then, and consequences to acting out were more strictly enforced. Plus, the majority of mothers didn't work outside the home; they had more hours to spend raising a child and smoothing out problems.

Contrast that with the looser family structures and the watered-down emphasis on social niceties that is prevalent in today's society. In many families, both parents work. Proper etiquette is no longer viewed as "essential" education as it once was. Social rules have relaxed, and "Miss Manners" has been replaced by a tolerance for individual expression, whether or not that expression is socially appropriate. I don't find many of these changes to be positive, but the scientist within me acknowledges that they are very real forces affecting our population.

These shifting, changing social rules (or lack thereof) make it more difficult for most people with autism to understand the social climate around them and learn to fit in. Many arrive at adulthood without even basic daily living capabilities—even children on the higher-functioning end of the spectrum. They can't make a sandwich, write a check, or use public transportation. Functional life skills have been neglected. Why that is, only each individual family can say for sure. But in general, this lack of attention to teaching basic life skills while children are young and growing is having increasingly negative repercussions on people with autism. Quirky friends I had in college, who would be diagnosed with mild autism today, all got and kept decent jobs because they had been taught basic social skills while they were growing up. They might still be quirky, still considered eccentric or even odd by some, but they could function within society.

One PhD I know is underemployed but has kept full-time jobs with full health benefits his entire life. In the meat industry where I work, there are older undiagnosed people with mild autism who have good jobs, with good pay, working as draftsmen, engineers, and mechanics. Their early upbringing gave them a foundation of basic skills, so they knew how to act socially, be part of a group, get along with others, etc. Today, I see younger individuals with autism who are just as intellectually bright getting fired for being regularly late to work or telling their bosses they won't do something required of their position. When I was little, I was expected to be on time and be ready for school, and I was. I had an alarm clock, and I set it every night. Things like getting up on time and bathing were basics that I had to do. Failure to live up to my parents' expectations resulted in a loss of privileges. My mother was good at making the consequences meaningful enough that I behaved. As I see it, some of the problems these teenagers and adults exhibit—being constantly defiant and not doing what the boss tells them—go back to not learning as children that compliance is required in certain situations. They never learned when they were six or eight that sometimes you have to do things that parents want you to do, such as going to church or having good table manners. You may not like it, but you still do it. There is one simple accommodation that would help autistic individuals keep jobs: replace sequential long verbal instructions from a boss to a checklist format. Each bullet point is either a task or a step in a task. It is similar to a pilot's checklist that all pilots are required to use. Research shows that autistic individuals have poor working memory, and the checklist creates an external working memory.

In light of this shifting sea of social skills and social expectations, how can parents and educators better prepare children to become independent, functioning adults while living in today's society? And what can we do to help the adults with autism who find themselves with adequate technical skills but are unemployable from a social perspective? We start by recognizing that changes need to be made. We need to be realistic with these individuals and our own roles in shaping their lives. We need to focus on talents rather than deficiencies.

Parents hold primary responsibility in making sure their children learn basic skills that will allow them to function within society as adults. This may sound harsh, but there's just no excuse for children growing into adults who can't do even basic things like set a table, wash their clothes, or handle money. We all make choices in our lives, and choosing to make the time for every child with autism to learn functional skills should be at the top of every parent's priority list. A child's future is at stake—and this should not be a negotiable item. Yet, for some reason, with a growing number of parents, that choice is not being made.

Our public education system also bears responsibility for preparing children to be independent adults. The needs of students with autism go beyond merely learning academics. They need to be taught to be flexible, social thinkers and understand group dynamics, and they need to be prepared to transition to adult life—whether or not that includes college or technical school—with functional life skills that neurotypicals learn almost by osmosis. Education of people with autism goes far beyond book learning. They absolutely require "life learning" also.

Develop Abilities into Employable Skills

Parents, educators, and teachers need to work on using an individual's areas of ability and interest and turn them into skills that other people want and appreciate. When I was eighteen, I talked constantly about cattle chutes. Other people did not want to hear me go on and on about the subject, but there was a very real need for people to design those cattle chutes. The adults in my life turned my obsession into the motivation for me to work hard, get my degree, and have a career in the cattle industry.

Teenagers with autism need to learn how to use their abilities to do work that other people value and need. When I was fifteen, I took care of nine horses and built many carpentry projects, such as the gate shown in the HBO movie *Temple Grandin*. The gate at my aunt's farm was manual and cumbersome. Without even being asked, I designed and built a gate that could be opened from a car. Teenagers must learn work skills that will help them succeed, such as using their artistic, writing, or musical abilities to do assigned tasks that produce something of value to another. A teenager with good writing skills could practice these work skills by writing a church bulletin or updating a church website. An individual who is good at art could do graphics for a local business or offer to paint with kids at a local community center or hospital.

Types of Thinking and Cognition

There are three different kinds of cognition. The *visual thinkers*, like me, who think in photo-realistic pictures, are good at jobs such as industrial design, graphics, photography, art, architecture, auto mechanics, and working with animals. I was terrible in algebra, and I am noticing more and more visual-thinking students with similar challenges. Many of these kids fail algebra and yet find higher math easy. They need to skip algebra and go right to geometry and trigonometry. I was never exposed to geometry because I failed algebra. Algebra is a barrier to many good careers. I have talked to many veterinary tech students who are failing their third algebra course. Both veterinarians and veterinary technicians seldom use algebra in their work. Recently I learned about a student who could not take the LSAT law exam because he failed algebra. Lawyers do not need algebra. For many careers, algebra should be replaced with either statistics or business math.

The music and math minds are *pattern thinkers* who are often good at music, engineering, computer programming, and statistics. Reading is often their weak area. The *verbal word thinkers* who love history are often good at jobs such as legal research, library science, journalism, and any job that requires good record keeping. One job they have excelled at is what I call, "Quiet specialized retail." Some examples would be selling cars, office supplies, business insurance, and financial products. They are appreciated for their specialized knowledge of the products. They help customers buy the right product that fits their needs. They tend to be really poor at drawing and visual skills. Most children will usually fit into one of these three categories, but there are a few who may not. Some kids have mixed learning styles, sitting halfway between the categories. One lady I know who falls into the music and math pattern thinking category understands music from a cognitive standpoint but is too uncoordinated to play an instrument. Many pattern thinkers see visual patterns in the relationship between numbers, but she does it all with sound patterns because she has almost no ability to think in photorealistic pictures the way I do. She has been employed for years doing computer programming.

I also want to emphasize that if a ninth grader is capable of doing university math, he should be encouraged to do it. A person with this advanced level of academic thinking who is forced to do the "baby math" of his peer group will quickly get bored and uncooperative. Focus on the areas of strength and develop them to their fullest expression. A child may be able to keep at grade level in one subject but may need special education in another. Autism is nothing if not variable.

Getting in the Back Door

Over the years, I have observed that some of the most successful people on the spectrum—those who found good jobs and kept their jobs—entered through the back door. They had parents or friends who recognized their talents and learning profiles and then capitalized on their strengths by teaching them a marketable skill, such as computer programming or auto mechanics. I got in the back door by showing potential clients pictures and drawings of cattle handling facilities I had designed. I went directly to the people who would appreciate my work. Had I started my job search in the traditional way, with the personnel office, I might never have been employed. Back then, my workplace social skills were underdeveloped, my personal hygiene was poor, and my temper flared regularly.

People respect true talent and demonstrated ability. A budding architect who brings in a fantastic building model or has a strong portfolio of projects he has completed will attract attention. Employers will become interested in working with people who have ability, even when they exhibit some social skills that are less than on par with their peers. The more specialized the talent, the more willing a potential employer may be to accommodate some differences. However, that is not the case for individuals with only marginal talents. That's why parents and educators need to focus on developing emerging talents to their fullest potential. This provides individuals with the best possible chance of securing a good job in their field, despite their social challenges.

The same principle applies to individuals who are on the more severe end of the spectrum. Many successful employment placements are made in local businesses that recognize the benefit of having an individual who will be a dependable, solid employee. People who are nonverbal know the difference between doing useful work that other people really need and appreciate, and stupid "busy work." One therapist could not figure out why her nonverbal client kept having a tantrum when she was teaching him to set the table. He was throwing a fit because he was asked to repeatedly set the table and then unset it, without ever eating. The therapist favored teaching skill acquisition over teaching functionality. A better way to teach table setting is to set the table, eat, and then clean up. All people want to feel their efforts matter, and individuals with autism are no different. We are learning that a lack of verbal communication does not always equate to impaired mental functioning. Even when it does, individuals can be trained to be contributing members of society. Some of the jobs suited to nonverbal persons are stocking shelves, jobs that involve sorting items, gardening work, landscaping, and some factory assembly jobs.

All individuals on the spectrum, from the brilliant scientist to the person who stocks shelves, find rapid multi-tasking difficult, if not impossible. If I had been a cashier in a busy restaurant, it would have been impossible to make change and talk to customers at the same time. Even today I have difficulty with multitasking and need to work through one thing at a time. For instance, I can't make breakfast, talk on the phone, and do laundry all at the same time. Parents and teachers, and persons with autism themselves, need to constantly look for the back door that will open up broader opportunities and employment options. Sometimes these chances can be right in front of you but you do not see them. My first entrance into a big meat plant came about when I met the wife of the plant's insurance agent. That one meeting became the connection I needed to get my foot in the (back) door.

Community colleges have all kinds of wonderful courses for different careers. Many students have found great teachers who served as mentors, both while they were in public school and afterward. Some parents of talented artists on the spectrum who cannot live independently took entrepreneurial courses so these parents could run a business selling their child's work.

Opportunities are available, with a little creative thought and a willingness to work outside the normal boundaries of education and employment.

Additional Reading

Grandin, T., and K. Duffy. 2004. *Developing Talents*. Shawnee Mission, KS: Autism Asperger Publishing Company.

Grandin, T., and Panek, R. 2013. *The Autistic Brain*. New York, NY: Houghton Mifflin Harcourt.

Grandin, T. (2023) *Visual Thinking: The Hidden Gifts of People Who Think in Pictures, Patterns, and Abstractions*, Penguin Random House, New York.

Harris, R. (2023) Trade school for autism gets new state-of-the-art facility. Denver News 7, Local news, January 13, 2023.

Martin, V. et al. (2022) Sustainable employment depends on the quality relationships between supervisors and their employees on the autism spectrum, *Disability and Rehabilitation*, 45(11):1784-1795.

Mottron, L. 2011. Changing perspectives: the power of autism. *Nature*. 479:34-35.

Schall, C. et al. (2020) The effect of business internships model and employment enhancing independence of young adults with significant impact of autism. *Intellectual and Developmental Disabilities*, 58(4):301-313.

Simone, R. 2010. *Asperger's on the Job*. Arlington, TX: Future Horizons.

Stand Together Foundation (2023) TACT Empowers the ASO community to use their gifts to succeed, Standtogetherfoundation.org.

VanBergeijk, E. et al. 2008. Supporting more able students on the autism spectrum: College and beyond. *Journal of Autism and Developmental Disorders* 38: 1359-1370.

Wehman, P.H., et al. 2013. Competitive employment for youth with autism spectrum disorders: early results from a randomized clinical trial. *Journal of Autism and Developmental Disorders* 44: 487-500.

Wehman, P.H, et.al. 2014. Project SEARCH for youth with autism spectrum disorders: increasing competitive employment on transition from high school. In press. *J Positive Behavior Interventions*.

IMPROVING TIME-MANAGEMENT AND ORGANIZATIONAL SKILLS

When I was in college, I did not have the time-management problems that are common for some individuals on the spectrum. Since I was motivated to succeed in college, I always got to class promptly and turned in homework on time. In this column I will discuss the ways I was able to succeed in school and life by having good time management and organizational skills.

Being on Time

In my life, being on time was emphasized from an early age. When I was a child, meals were served on a set schedule, and I was expected to be back from a friend's house in time for dinner. Every Sunday, my family went to church and I had to be dressed in my Sunday best on time. By the time I got to college, being on time for class and getting up in the morning was easy.

A teenager should start learning how to be on time and get up early before he or she goes to college. This skill could be taught by having the teenager do a job such as walking the next-door neighbor's dog at eight in the morning. This would teach the discipline of being up on time for an 8:00 AM class. Taking classes at a local community college will be much easier if being on time is learned before enrollment.

Turning in Assignments on Time

I never waited until close to the deadline to study for an exam or turn in a term paper. Each day I set aside time to study and keep up. My term papers were always done way before the deadline. I finished my papers early to ensure a quality job. Doing them early also helped me avoid missing deadlines because of last-minute problems such as getting sick.

Scheduling Time to Work and Study

For me, the best types of calendars show one month on a single sheet of paper. I like this type of calendar because I can see the entire month. Monthly calendars are also available in an electronic format. For some individuals, a smartphone has been useful for keeping organized.

On a monthly calendar, I recorded times for exams and due dates for term papers. I set aside large blocks of time for collecting research material I would need for a term paper. For writing papers, I scheduled time in blocks of two to four hours so I could really concentrate on the assignment. I could get my work done more efficiently and quickly by scheduling fewer big blocks of time compared to scheduling many little blocks. I always scheduled time to study for exams, and I often tutored weak students as a method of studying. I never crammed for exams all night.

Organizational Skills

In the 1960s when I went to college, most students had a large loose-leaf binder for keeping all their class notes. This type of binder solved many organizational problems. I had one of these binders, and I never lost class notes.

To keep track of my class notes, I had to have them all in one place. This prevented me from losing them on my messy desk.

At the beginning of each semester, I bought a new binder for my classes. After my four years in college, I had eight binders with the notes for all my courses. Referring back to previous courses was useful and easy to do. It may be old-fashioned, but using a binder is the best way to keep handwritten class notes organized. It is helpful to use a colored tab divider for each class. You can keep a class schedule in the front of the binder.

Today, fewer students use this type of loose-leaf binder. If notes are taken on a laptop, I recommend having an icon on the desktop for class notes, and then a separate file folder for each class.

One of the best ways to help a student be successful in college is to work on time management and organizational skills while he or she is still in high school. It is never too early to start teaching these important life skills. If an individual has not been taught these skills, it is never too late to start. People on the spectrum can always keep learning.

Use a Checklist Like an Airline Pilot

I have difficulty remembering a sequence of tasks if they are given to me verbally. I need to make a list of the tasks that I can keep on a piece of paper, like a pilot's checklist. The list could also be put on a smartphone. For example, the list might include the steps to take apart, clean, and reassemble a coffee or ice cream machine in a restaurant.

EMPLOYMENT ADVICE: TIPS FOR GETTING AND HOLDING A JOB

Grooming

When you first meet with a prospective employer, dress neatly. Your hair should be combed and your clothes must be clean. When I got my first job at a cattle feedlot construction company, I was a slob. Fortunately, my boss recognized my talents and had his secretaries work with me on grooming. Not everyone will be that fortunate; make sure you have good grooming skills.

Sell Your Work

I got my first job because the technical people at the company were impressed with my ability to design cattle-handling equipment. Many people with autism do poorly at a job interview with the personnel department. You need to locate the technical people and show them a portfolio of your work. In the 1970s, when I was just getting started with my cattle equipment design business, I always carried with me a portfolio of pictures and drawings.

Today it is easy to have your portfolio always available on a smartphone or tablet computer. I had to carry a large notebook, but today I could have drawings and pictures of completed projects on a phone. Always having the portfolio with you makes it possible to have it available when you meet the right person who can open the door to employment.

I started my freelance design business with one small project at a time. I got additional design projects because my designs worked and people noticed my talent. Starting small and building my business slowly worked for me.

People respect talent. You need to be trained in an employable field, such as computer programming, drafting, or accounting. The technical professions offer more opportunities for employment and are overall well suited to the autism/AS style of thinking. Show a prospective employer a portfolio of computer programs or engineering drawings, or a sample of complex accounting projects. It will help. Or go freelance yourself. Many local businesses would like to hire a computer person to come to their business every month to keep their computers running smoothly. Many people who run a home-based business would also like this type of help, since they're usually too busy running the business to do these types of tasks. This would be a perfect freelance business for a person with autism who has strong technical know-how.

Dependability

You need to be punctual and show up for work on time. That also goes for being on time for scheduled meetings during office hours. Employers value dependable employees.

Visual Difficulties at Work

Some people with autism have difficulty tolerating fluorescent lights or LEDs that flicker. Sometimes wearing a hat with a big brim or baseball hat is helpful. They can see the sixty-cycle flicker of the lights, and it makes the office environment flash like a disco. Now that most lights are LED's, some people can see flicker on certain LED's. LEDs can be tested for flickering by photographing a room in slow-motion video. If a workspace has no windows and flickering LEDs, an autistic employee should find a bright LED that does not flicker and put it in their workstation Some flat-screen computer monitors may flicker, and others do not. Sometimes flickering can be stopped by increasing the refresh rate. Laptops and tablets never flicker, and they could be substituted for a desktop computer.

Some people find reading easier if they print text on tan, gray, light blue, or other pastel paper to reduce contrast. They can also try different pale-colored backgrounds and different fonts on their computer.

Sound Sensitivity Problems at Work

The noise and commotion of a factory or office are sometimes a problem for people with sound sensitivity. You may want to ask that your desk be located in a quieter part of the office. Headphones or earplugs can help, but you must not wear them all the time. Earplugs worn all the time may make the ears more sensitive, so they must be removed when you get home.

Autism Has Slow Brain Processing Speed

Autistic people have the advantage of having a great ability for detailed memory, but this kind of brain processes information more slowly. Slow processing speed can cause the following difficulties:

1. Understanding rapid conversation in highly social situations.
2. Jobs that require rapid multi-tasking, such as a busy take-out window. These types of jobs should be avoided.
3. Giving a rapid response to a question.

4. Remembering long strings of verbal instructions. This is why a pilot's checklist format should be used for many tasks. Recent research clearly shows working memory problems and slower processing speed are problems for autistic individuals (Rabiec et al., 2020; Zapparrata et al., 2023).

5. Problems with interrupting conversation. Slow processing speed makes it difficult to detect gaps in the conversation.

Diplomacy

I learned some hard lessons about being diplomatic when I had my first interactions with people at work. Some senior engineers designed a project that contained some mistakes that were obvious to me. Not knowing any better, I wrote a letter to their boss, citing in great detail the errors in their design and calling them "stupid." It was not well received. You simply cannot tell other people they are stupid, even if they really are stupid. Just do your job and never criticize your boss or other employees.

Freelance Work

This is often a good way to work because it avoids many of the social problems. When I design equipment, I can go into the plant, get the project done, and then leave before I get involved in complex workplace politics. The internet makes freelancing much easier. If you can find a boss who recognizes both your strengths and social limitations, this will make life on the job much easier.

Being Too Good

Several people with autism have told me that they got into trouble with coworkers at a factory because they were "too good" at assembling "widgets." The problem of employee jealousy is a difficult thing to understand, but it exists in the workplace. The boss likes the hard worker, but the other employees may hate him or her. If coworkers do get jealous of your work, I found that it is helpful to try to find something they have built or done that you can genuinely compliment them on. It helps them feel appreciated and that they, too, have done a good job.

Avoid the Peter Principle

The Peter principle states that people have a tendency to rise to their level of incompetence. There have been several sad cases where a good draftsman, lab technician, or journalist with autism has been promoted into management, and then fired because the social situations got too complex. The person with autism is especially vulnerable to being promoted into a job they cannot handle because of the social issues. It may be best to politely tell your boss that you can use your skills best in your present position.

Be Nice and Have Good Manners

People who are polite and cheerful will have an easier time getting along at work. Make sure you always say "please" and "thank you." Good table manners are a must. Greet your fellow workers at least once each day and actively try to engage in some small talk with the people you work with most closely.

While it's not necessary to form friendships with everyone you work with, some social interaction is needed if you are to be viewed as part of the group.

Workplace Politics

One of the hardest lessons I had to learn when I entered the workplace is that some people in a company had personal agendas other than doing their best work. For some, it was to climb the corporate ladder and achieve some high-level position. For others, it was to do the least amount of work possible without getting fired. Another rule I learned is to avoid discussing controversial subjects at work. Sex, religion, and political affiliations are subjects that should not be discussed at work. You can easily alienate people or give them cause to dislike you when you overstep these boundaries. You may hear other employees talking about these subjects; let them. Keep in mind that the "hidden social rules" in doing so are massive, and spectrum individuals usually miss most of them. Safe subjects are pets, sports, electronics, weather, hobbies, and popular TV shows and movies that avoid these sensitive areas. Workplace politics are not easy to understand; just realize that they exist. Try to stay out of it, unless it directly jeopardizes your job or affects your ability to perform your job.

Additional Reading

Rabiec, A. et al. (2020) Working memory deficits and its relationship to autism spectrum disorder, *Iranian Journal of Medical Science*, 45(2):100-109.

Zapparrata, N. et al. (2023) Slower processing speed in autism spectrum disorder. A meta-analytic investigation of time-based tasks, *Journal of Autism and Developmental Disorders*, 53(12):4618-4640.

TEENS WITH AUTISM MUST LEARN BOTH SOCIAL AND WORK SKILLS TO KEEP JOBS

I have been seeing too many teenagers and young adults in their twenties who have never learned any job-related social skills or the discipline to do the work assigned to them. This greatly interferes with their ability to get and keep jobs. An individual must not only learn the skills of a trade but also must know how to work with others. Many individuals manage to get a job and then fail to keep it because they have never learned the discipline of teamwork and working hard. Even self-employed people must know how to work with others, or they won't have a job for long. Too many individuals who have much milder symptoms than mine are ending up collecting Social Security disability payments.

One may wonder where all the undiagnosed older people with mild autism or the new DSM-5 diagnosis of social communication disorder are.

I see these people all the time in my work in the livestock industry. They are the old hippie who runs the maintenance shop at a meat plant, the guy who runs the computer department, or a person who is a really good welder. These older undiagnosed people on the milder end of the spectrum have kept their jobs because they learned both work skills and social skills. For some of these older individuals, a paper route was the best thing that ever happened to them. Paper routes taught the discipline of work and the reward of earning money. Today the paper routes are gone, but a twelve-year-old could walk dogs for two or three of the neighbors, fix computers, shop for older people, work at a family business, or be a museum tour guide. Parents need to set up opportunities for learning to work, through neighbors and friends. It is important that the job involves working for other people, outside the home. Volunteer work is also effective, but it needs to be on a regular schedule. Some examples that could be easily set up in the neighborhood are setting up chairs every weekend at the local church, working at a farmer's market, or making snacks for different events in the community.

It's Never Too Early!

Sewing. At age thirteen, I worked two afternoons a week for a local seamstress who did freelance sewing out of her house. Mother set up this job for me. I hemmed dresses and took apart garments. The main thing I learned from this job was I got rewarded with money because I did the job right.

Working with animals. At age fifteen, I cleaned horse stalls every day at the boarding school I attended and took care of the school's horses. I got this job because I took the initiative to just start doing it. Others were more than happy to let me do it. I often get asked, "What motivated you?" I was motivated by the sense of accomplishment and the recognition I received working in the horse barn as a volunteer job. Gradually, the job morphed into managing the horse barn. During the summer, mother arranged for me to develop further work skills at my aunt's ranch.

Carpentry and designing signs. At boarding school, at around age sixteen or seventeen, I was encouraged when I expressed an interest in doing carpentry work on our ski tow house. I installed tongue-and-groove wood siding with white trim. Other projects I completed were shingling the barn roof and making signs for events such as the winter carnival. From this experience I learned how to make products that other people would like. I had to make a sign that was appropriate for our school's winter carnival. This was a volunteer job, and I enjoyed the recognition for making something that other people appreciated.

College internships. I completed two summer internships arranged by my mother and the staff at Franklin Pierce College. One summer I worked with children with autism. The next summer, I worked in a research lab and had to rent a house and share it with another person. My roommate and I often cooked together and ate the same things for supper. She loved liver, and I ate it even though I did not like it. On another night, we ate something that I liked. This was an extension of the turn-taking I had learned from playing board games as a young child.

Magazine writing and design work. During my childhood, I had lots of practice talking to adults. When I was eight, Mother had me dress up in my Sunday best and shake hands and introduce myself to her dinner guests. I also served the snacks during the cocktail hour. I was the greeter and snack server every time Mother had friends over for dinner. When I went to Arizona State University to get my master's degree, I already had the entrepreneurial spirit. I had the confidence to walk up to people and show them my work. The HBO movie *Temple Grandin* shows me walking up to the editor of the *Arizona Farmer Rancher* and getting his card. I actually did this. This is how I got my first article in the magazine. This is an alternative to the usual job application process—which has worked for me.

My design business started the same way. It was one small project at a time. When people saw my drawings, they were impressed. It was tons of hard work, and it was not easy. But what really helped me was that I had learned how to work and how to get along with others at my previous jobs.

It's Never Too Late!

I want to emphasize that it is never too late to help your child learn these vital skills. Recently, I met a mother whose son was undiagnosed, and the family called him "Sammy who is different." His mother made him get up every morning and get out the door to work. She had to push him. She wondered if she would have pushed him as hard if he had been Asperger's Sammy. Today he is in his thirties and has a career he loves.

Teachers and parents need to "stretch" individuals on the milder end of the spectrum. To develop my abilities and social skills, I had to be pushed just outside my comfort zone. One word of caution: the activities that stretched and helped me to develop were never a sudden surprise. Remember that surprises can cause panic and fear for individuals on the spectrum. Be sure to prepare the person for the experiences that will help them achieve long-time job success!

Developing a skill into an employable position will take lots of work and more training for people with autism. However, once they succeed, they will become excellent employees.

But they must avoid being promoted from a position they can handle well to a management position they cannot handle.

HAPPY PEOPLE ON THE AUTISM SPECTRUM HAVE SATISFYING JOBS OR HOBBIES

In my travels to many autism meetings, I have observed that fully autistic people who make the best adjustments in life are the ones who have satisfying jobs. A job that uses a person's intellectual abilities is great for improving self-esteem. Conversely, the most unhappy people on the spectrum I have met are those who did not develop a good employable skill or a hobby they can share with others. With so much of adult life spent in our jobs, it makes sense that people with satisfying jobs will generally be happier with their lives and better able to respond to different situations that may arise. Grant South and Naomi Sutherland, Griffith University in Australia, found enabling special interests and making them productive was important. They emphasized using a strength-based approach.

I have met several successful people on the spectrum who program computers. One autistic computer programmer told me she was happy because now she is with "her people." At another meeting, I met a father and son. The father had taught his son computer programming. He started teaching him when he was in the fourth grade, and now he works at a computer company. For many people with autism, the way our mind works is well-suited to this profession. Parents and teachers should capitalize on this ability and encourage its development.

Several years ago, I visited autism programs in Japan. I met a large number of fully verbal autistic people. Every one of them was employed in a good job.

One man translated technical and legal documents. Another person was an occupational therapist, and there were several computer programmers. One man who was somewhat less verbal works as a baker. What I noticed is that the attitude in Japan is to develop skills. These people with autism benefited from that attitude, and would for the rest of their lives.

In designing livestock equipment, I have worked with many welding shops. About 20 percent of the people were undiagnosed autistic, dyslexic, or ADHD. Several of them had multiple patents. Today there is a shortage of highly skilled tradespeople. The autistic person who would love fixing elevators may be in the basement playing video games because they were never exposed to fixing mechanical things. Recently, I almost got stuck in an elevator that had not been serviced.

While developing an inherent skill into an employable position can be work, it is necessary for people with autism/AS to try hard to do this. However, once they succeed, they must be careful to avoid being promoted from a technical position they can handle well to a management position they cannot handle. I have heard several sad stories of successful people being promoted out of jobs they were good at. These people had jobs such as draftsman, lab technician, sportswriter, and computer programmer. Once they were required to interact socially as part of their management position, their performance suffered.

Hobbies where people have shared interests are also great in building self-esteem. I read about a woman who was unhappy in a dead-end job. Her life turned around when she discovered that there were other people in the world also interested in her hobby. In her spare time, she breeds fancy chickens. Through the internet, she communicates with other chicken breeders.

Because she explored her hobby, she is now much happier, even though she still works at her dead-end job. In my opinion, using the internet for communicating with other hobbyists is much more constructive than gripping with other people on the spectrum on the internet. That doesn't benefit anyone.

Parents and teachers need to place a priority on discovering and then developing the many skills that people with autism possess. These skills can be turned into careers and hobbies that will provide shared interests with other people.

For an autistic person to become interested in a job, they have to be exposed to it. Many kids today grow up without using tools. The pathway to good jobs starts with exposure and then mentoring. All kids need to experience many things to determine both what they like and what they can be good at.

Effect of Artificial Intelligence (AI) on Jobs

If a job is hands-on, it will not be taken over by artificial intelligence. Nurses and elevator repair people are not going to be replaced by AI. The jobs most at risk of getting replaced by AI are translation, video game animation, low-level programming such as web design, copy editing, accounting, and some graphic design jobs. Live theater and live concerts will not be replaced. People will still want to see real people. There was a Broadway show with autistic lead actors, titled *How to Dance in Ohio*. I saw the show, and they did a great job. I wrote this section when I was on an airplane. Major portions of the airplane were built in a factory that Boeing foolishly sold to a private equity company. The one person I would totally trust to tighten the bolts on the rudder would be autistic. If this is done wrong, the pilot might have difficulty steering the plane. My worst nightmare would be an AI system owned by private equity supervising an airplane factory.

INSIDE OR OUTSIDE?
THE AUTISM CULTURE

A frequent topic of discussion within the autism community is how much people with autism should have to adapt to the world of the neurotypicals. My view is that you should still be yourself, but you will have to make some changes in your behavior, too. Years ago, Dr. Leo Kanner, the person who first described autism, stated that the people who made the best adaptation to the world realized themselves that they had to make some behavioral changes.

This was true for me, too. In 1974, I was hired by a feedlot construction company. My boss made it very clear to me that I had to improve my grooming. I dressed like a slob and paid very little attention to my grooming habits. With the help of some of the secretaries, I learned to dress better, and I worked conscientiously to have better personal hygiene. In the HBO movie, my boss slammed a can of deodorant on the table in front of me and said, "You stink." This really happened to me, and at the time, I was furious. Today, I thank that boss for forcing me to change. It made me more socially accepted. For me, it was a logical process; it followed the *if/then* sequence of a computer code. *If* I wanted my job, *then* I had to change these behaviors. So I did.

Even today, I do not dress the way everybody else does. I like to wear Western clothes; they are my way of expressing myself. Dressing in a distinct way like this is acceptable; being a dirty slob is not.

I think it is OK to be eccentric. There are many geeky eccentric people who are very successful in many fields. Silicon Valley is full of brilliant people who look and act differently, like the geek Sheldon character in the television series *The Big Bang Theory*. (If you've never watched this show, do so. The four main characters all have social challenges in various ways, and this series can be used to discuss social problems and solutions with an individual on the spectrum.) Many people with strong eccentricities are likely to be on the milder end of the autism spectrum. As long as you're good at what you do, being eccentric is often overlooked or accepted by others. This is not the case if the talent level is mediocre or poor.

One time I talked to a lady with AS who liked to wear plastic, see-through dresses made in bright Day-Glo colors. Her employer really frowned upon this. She told me that wearing these dresses was part of being who she was. While I understood her desire to retain her individuality, I pointed out to her that her dresses might be okay at a party, but they were inappropriate attire for a work environment. Unless she compromised, her job would be in jeopardy. I suggested a toned-down version of her outfits that would be more socially acceptable at work, such as wearing a conventional dress and decorating it with a few Day-Glo accessories, such as a belt, purse, or earrings.

Techies versus Suits: The Corporate World

In the corporate world, there is constant friction between technical people, such as computer programmers and engineers, and managers. The tech staff often refer to managers as "suits" (but we don't say this to their faces). Many technical people in large industries have mild autism traits. To them, technical things are interesting and social things are boring. Some of the best times in my life have been spent with other engineers and techies discussing how to build meat plants. The technical people are my social world. We share common personality and behavior traits that provide us with common ground for discussion and help us better understand each other. (It is also great fun to talk about how most "suits" would be incapable of making a paper bag.)

Every big corporation in a technical field has its department of social misfits who make the place run. Even a bank has some purely technical people who handle accounting, fix ATMs, and run the computers. There is no black-and-white dividing line between computer nerds or geeks with fully verbal autism. And there will always be friction between the techies and the suits. The suits are the highly social verbal people who rise to the top and become managers. However, they would have nothing to sell and no business to run if they lost all their techies. Both the techies and the suits need each other. Every tech start-up, when it gets to be a certain size, has to hire a suit to run the business. The business needs a highly verbal "suit" to keep the operation organized.

Parents, teachers, or others who involve themselves with people with autism/AS need to realize that you cannot turn a nonsocial animal into a social one. Your focus should be teaching people with autism to adapt to the social world around them, while still retaining the essence of who they are, including their autism. Learning social survival skills is important, but I cannot be something I am not. But efforts to enlarge the social world of teens and adults with autism should follow a different path. Rather than focus on their deficiencies, it's better to focus on their abilities and find creative ways to capitalize on their strengths to bring them more into social situations.

Some of the bright, socially awkward teenagers need to be removed from the torture chamber of high school and enrolled in technical classes at a community college. This will enable them to be with their true intellectual peers, in fields such as cybersecurity, electronics, welding, electrical, and other pursuits. They need to choose a career that will not be replaced by AI. Recently, I looked at the catalogue from a community college, and all the different, fascinating technical courses would have been great for me in high school.

Some people with autism think in very rigid patterns and see a particular behavior in an all-or-nothing manner. When we are asked, or expected, to change a behavior, we think that means we need to extinguish it. Most times, that is not the case. It is more that we need to modify the behavior and understand the times and places when it is acceptable or not. For instance, I can still dress like a slob in my own home, when no one else is around (a trait I've learned is shared with many neurotypicals). Finding a way to compromise so that we keep our personal nature but conform to some of the unspoken rules of society (including the workplace) is where our efforts need to be.

Additional Reading

Silberman, S. 2015. *NeuroTribes: The Legacy of Autism and the Future of Neurodiversity*, Avery Books Penguin Random House, New York, NY.

PORTFOLIOS CAN OPEN JOB AND COLLEGE OPPORTUNITIES

Individuals with autism need to get creative and find ways to discover employment or educational opportunities without going through the traditional front-door route of interviews or entrance exams. I never sold a single design job in my cattle equipment design business by doing an interview; I sold jobs by showing a portfolio of my work to the managers of packing plants and feedlots. I learned early in my career that if I showed drawings and photos of my work to the right person, I could get a job.

When I was first starting out, everybody thought I was a weird nerd, but I got respect when I showed off my drawings. I got into the Swift & Company meat plant in the early 1970s because I met a lady who liked the shirt I had embroidered by hand. She turned out to be the wife of the plant's insurance agent. I was wearing my portfolio, and I did not realize it! You never know where you may meet the person who can open the door for you.

Put Your Portfolio on Your Phone

With today's smartphones, it is really easy for the individual with autism, as well as their parents and teachers, to carry a portfolio. The portfolio can contain pictures of art, drawings, a rebuilt classic car, computer programming, samples of creative writing, mathematics, and many other things. In many situations, there is a back door, but many people fail to see it. One secret is networking with the right person. That person could be a retired engineer, a lady in the choir, or the man in line at the supermarket checkout aisle. This is why your portfolio must always be with you. Countless times I have had young people on the spectrum tell me that they have been turned away at the "front door." I have talked to many talented individuals, but most of them failed to have their portfolio with them, or their portfolio was messy, with poor work mixed in with their good work.

Technology Is a Back Door

The secret is to show either your own work or your child's work to the right person. Today's social networks, such as Facebook and LinkedIn, make it even easier to find the person who can open the back door and circumvent the front-door interview or admissions process. Wikipedia has a list of social networking websites. Use the keywords *social networking websites* to locate appropriate sites.

Access Higher Education

Kristine Barnett, a mother of a young boy with autism, found that her son was going nowhere in a special education classroom. He was bored and exhibited challenging behaviors. She started taking him to a local observatory, where he could look through a telescope and listen to fascinating lectures. She bought him advanced books on astronomy, and he learned algebra in elementary school. Kristine recognized the need to keep Jake in a regular elementary school class so he could learn social skills. To prevent boredom, he was allowed to read his higher-level math books when the other children were doing arithmetic. When Jake was eight, Kristine called an astronomy professor at the local university and asked if Jake could sit in on a lecture. Jake impressed the professor with his knowledge, and other professors became interested in him. Jake quickly advanced through college math and physics classes. Today he is a theoretical physicist at the Peremiles Institute in Waterloo, Ontario, Canada. Jake's story is an excellent example of getting in the back door.

Make It Easy for Others to Help

Every week I receive numerous inquiries from people on the spectrum, parents, and teachers who are begging for help. The problem is that many of them make it difficult for me to reach them. I get letters where the only address contact information is on the envelope, and I cannot read it. I get emails that do not work, or they do not have phone numbers and postal addresses. You must include complete information if you want to get through to a busy person. You need to make it easy to contact you. Correspondence is often answered on weekends by busy people, so give out your cell phone number. Due to viruses, many people will not open a strange email attachment, so you need to establish contact via phone or email first.

After seeing a person's strong portfolio, a top professor in math, art, physics, or creative writing who believes in that student will find a way to get him into the university even though that student may have failed in other academic areas. Individuals have been accepted into good college programs because they showed their portfolio to the right professors. This approach has also worked with skilled trade jobs. I worked with a drafting technician who got a job by showing off a homework assignment from his one-semester computer video and drafting class. The portfolio has to be shown to the right person. Showing it to the human resources department would be useless because they would not appreciate the drawing. Showing it to the right person in the engineering department got him the job.

Additional Reading

Barnett, Kristine. 2013. *The Spark: A Mother's Story of Nurturing Genius*. New York: Random House.

"What happened to Jacob Barnett? Where is Jacob Barnett Now?" Fresherlive.com

GOING TO COLLEGE: TIPS FOR PEOPLE WITH AUTISM

Going off to college can be an unnerving experience for people with autism. Usually, the high level of help that parents and teachers provide during middle and high school just drops off, and the person can find the transition difficult at best. In this column, I'll share some tips I learned from my college experience.

Teasing

When I was in high school, being teased was torture. Teenagers were hyper-social beings I did not understand. I think that some autistic students who are capable of doing college-level work need to be removed from the difficult high school scene. Let them take a few courses at a community college or university. Parents often ask about age restrictions at the college; I learned a long time ago it is better not to ask. Just sign up the student.

Tutors and Mentors

I had a great science teacher when I was in high school. When the teasing became unbearable, I did science projects in Mr. Carlock's lab. He was one often there to help me when I enrolled in college. Having the same mentor in both high school and college was a tremendous help. I have talked to many students who failed several classes and dropped out of school because they did not seek help or tutoring when they started having trouble with a subject.

Seek help at the first sign of trouble. When I had difficulty with math and French classes, I found people to tutor me. It made the difference between me failing and succeeding.

Uneven Skills

Many people on the autism continuum have uneven skills. They do well in some subjects and poorly in others. Tutoring may be needed in some subjects. It also may be a good idea to take a lighter course load.

Living at College

My first room assignment in college was with two other roommates. This was a disaster. I could not sleep and had no peace and quiet. I was then moved to a room with one roommate. This was a much better arrangement. Several of the roommates and I became good friends. A person with autism needs a quiet place to live. I recommend visiting the campus before enrolling to make the transition easier.

Campus Clubs

I was active in several campus organizations where I was able to use my skills and talents. People appreciate talent, and being good at something helps compensate for being weird. When the college put on a musical variety show, I made many of the sets. I also made signs and posters for the ski club and the social committee. At the 2024 Northern California neurodiversity and disability conference at the University of California, Chico, a panel of college students emphasized the importance of joining clubs and participating in events organized by their academic departments. These activities helped them make social connections through shared interests.

Tips on Classes

I always sat in the front row so I could hear better. It is sometimes difficult for me to hear hard consonant sounds. After class, I always recopied all my notes to help me learn the material. Fluorescent lights or LEDs did not bother me, but many people with autism cannot tolerate them. The room will appear to flash on and off like a disco, which makes learning during a lecture difficult. Some students have found that placing a lamp with an LED that does not flicker on their desk may block the flicker from the ceiling lights. The worst LED lights can be located by taking pictures with slow-motion video. Wearing a baseball cap with a long visor helps make the fluorescent ceiling lights more tolerable. Audio-record the lecture so it can be listened to later in a room without distractions.

Smaller colleges and college classes may be a better choice for some students with autism. I went to a small college that had small classes. That was a real benefit, as it gave me better access to my instructors and removed the intense sensory problems of a large classroom with hundreds of people. For some students, taking the first two years of classes at a community college may help prevent them from being overwhelmed by college experiences, and either dropping out or flunking out.

Behavior in Class

There are certain behaviors that are expected of students while they are in a classroom setting. Often these "unwritten rules" are not taught to a student before college. Two big classroom behavior no-nos are monopolizing the teacher's time and disrupting the class. For instance, I had a rule that I could ask a maximum of two questions per class period. I know of many spectrum students who will monopolize a teacher's time with an endless stream of questions, or who will interrupt others who are speaking in class to challenge what they are saying. These are both inappropriate behaviors. Others include making excessive noise while others are trying to concentrate (like during an exam), texting on a cell phone during class, listening to music on earphones during class, etc. Spectrum students who are not aware of these hidden rules can ask the instructor or a fellow classmate for some help. Don't assume you know these rules innately.

Grooming Skills

You have to learn not to be a slob. Ideally, good hygiene skills should be learned before you go to college. Many grooming activities such as shaving cause sensory discomfort. The person should try different shavers until they find one they can tolerate. It is often more comfortable to use unscented, hypoallergenic deodorant and cosmetics.

Choice of College Major or Technical School Field

One problem I have observed is that a person with autism gets through college and then is unable to get a job. It is important that the person majors in a field that will make them employable. Some good majors are engineering, industrial design (that's my field), architecture, construction, computer science, veterinary technology (vet nurse), nursing, library science, and special education. For people going to a community college or technical school, take courses such as architectural drafting or computer programming, or a trade such as electrician, welding, or auto mechanics. Get really good at your skill. People respect talent. Artificial intelligence will eliminate many jobs, such as computer animation and accounting. I am emphasizing the hands-on jobs because they will not be replaced by artificial intelligence. I had problems with math, so I had to avoid majoring in engineering, because I could not do algebra. My major in psychology and animal science had much lower math requirements.

Transition from College to Work

Individuals with autism should start working part-time in their chosen field before they leave college. A slow transition from college to employment will be easier. While still in college, do career-relevant work each summer, even if it has to be on a volunteer basis. During my college years, I worked on my aunt's ranch, in a research lab, and at a summer program for children with autism. I am seeing too many talented people graduating from college who have never held a job of any kind. It is this lack of job experience that makes it difficult for them to find employment after college. They have no experience in being in a work environment, having to do tasks that other people assign, working alongside other people and the social requirements of doing so, or organizing their time and their workload, etc.

FINDING MENTORS AND APPROPRIATE COLLEGES

O ver the years, many people have asked me, "How did you find the mentors who helped you?" Mentors did, indeed, play a pivotal role in helping me become the person and professional I am today. They can be valuable catalysts to helping the spectrum child or teen learn fundamental study and research skills that will propel them toward a future career.

Mentors are attracted to ability. Many people will become interested in mentoring a child if they are shown examples of what the child is capable of doing. Portfolios of artwork, math, or writing can entice a potential mentor. A mentor can sometimes be found in the most unlikely places. He or she could be a retired engineer you sing beside in the church choir or a colleague at work.

When I was an inferior student in high school, my science teacher, Mr. Carlock, saved me by getting me interested in science. Our relationship started quite unexpectedly. The other teachers asked Mr. Carlock to talk to me because I was doing kind of "crazy talk" about the meaning of life. He explained that many of the ideas the other teachers thought were crazy were similar to the thoughts of well-known philosophers. He gave me books written by David Hume and other philosophers to whet my appetite to learn. After grabbing my interest this way, his next step was to motivate me to change my poor performance in class. He did this by saying, "If you want to find out why your squeeze machine is relaxing, you will need to study to become a scientist." He then took me to a big library to learn how real scientists search for journal articles. I read article after article about sensory perception. The library skills he taught me transferred easily to finding information on the internet. This is a good example of using my fixations to motivate my interest in schoolwork.

Parents, teachers, and friends need to always be on the lookout for possible mentors. Many retired individuals would love to work with a high school kid. Several individuals on the autism spectrum have gone into successful technical careers after being mentored by a retired person. It does not matter if the mentor's skills are old. What a mentor does is get a student turned on to learning. There is a discipline to learning a skill such as graphic design or computer programming. Once the mentor gets the student turned on, a spectrum person will go to the bookstore or the internet and buy the manuals to learn the modern techniques. I have observed that most teenagers on the autism spectrum need the discipline of formal instruction to get started. This is especially true in learning good study habits, researching information, and other related executive functioning skills, such as time management, group project strategies, etc.

Finding the Right College

I often get asked about colleges for individuals on the spectrum. There's no easy, quick answer to this question. I went to a small school—Franklin Pierce College in New Hampshire. Mother talked to the dean, and they were willing to work with me. There are lots of small two-year and four-year colleges. A small school was ideal for my freshman and sophomore year because it avoided the problem of becoming lost in huge classes. The best approach is to identify a few schools that "fit" the person's needs and then look for specific people in an institution who are willing to help.

Recently I have been doing a lot of talks at both large and small colleges. One school had an extensive department for helping students with disabilities, and another small school emphasized hands-on learning in ecology and sustainable agriculture. The type of learning environments that appeal to the autistic way of thinking are often available. However, you need to seek out specific professors or counselors at both the community colleges and the four-year schools to help your child get in. Send a professor a portfolio of the student's work. One girl with autism got into a top-ranked school after she sent her poetry to an English professor. You need to look for the "back door"—a professor who likes a student's work can let the student in.

To find an appropriate college, start your search on the internet. I typed in "colleges in Ohio," "colleges in Oregon," and "colleges in Alabama." I was amazed at the huge number of colleges in each state. Every college has a webpage and sub-webpages for each department, which usually offer a list of faculty. When I went to the University of Illinois, I was interested in the work of a specific professor because I had been reading his journal articles. The next step was visiting the university and talking to two professors about my interests. They admitted me to the graduate program, even though my standardized test scores were poor, because they were intrigued by my research ideas.

Being recognized in the cattle industry for my ability to design systems that worked was an added plus. Think creatively and find a back door into the college that is a good match for your child. A strong portfolio or an interesting idea for a research project may be the key. It's never too soon to start; the time to click the mouse is now.

When an individual with autism graduates and gets out into the world of employment, it is often much wiser not to fully disclose.

REASONABLE ACCOMMODATION FOR INDIVIDUALS ON THE AUTISM SPECTRUM

I received an email recently from a woman with autism who is successfully partway through a PhD program. She was inspired by my story and decided to get over her "handicapped mentality" and not let autism stand in the way of success. I am becoming more and more concerned about young students who are using autism as an excuse not to be able to do certain things. My mother insisted on standards of behavior such as good table manners, patient turn-taking, and not being rude. It is never too late to start teaching the essential social skills whether a person is two, twelve, or twenty.

In my opinion, some of the accommodations students are asking for in college are ridiculous and promote the handicapped mentality. One student expected the counseling department at a large university to intervene and stop a student who was using his mobile phone to text message in a huge class filled with over two hundred students. To solve this problem, all she had to do was change seats to get away from the clicking keys. No one had taught her how to look for a simple solution first.

I have been receiving increasing complaints from college professors about students who disrupt classes and attempt to converse with the professor during class. When I was in college, I had a rule that I could ask a maximum of two questions per class period. Mr. Carlock, my science teacher, explained that the reason for this rule is to provide other students an opportunity to ask their questions. The principle is the same as turn-taking during board games or card games.

However, there are reasonable accommodations that are essential for some autistic individuals in college. A student may need just one or most of these accommodations.

- Taking exams in a room without fluorescent lights or LED lights that flicker. I had a dyslexic student who totally "spaced out" and could not think in a room with fluorescent lights. Bad LEDs that flicker can be located by taking slow-motion video of a classroom.
- Some extra time on tests.
- A quiet place to study; some individuals may need a private dorm room.
- Tutoring in some subjects.
- A lighter course load and taking an extra year to finish the degree.
- Making checklists and visual schedules. I used a printed-out monthly calendar where the due dates for different assignments could be written down. It helped me to be able to see the whole month.

At my university, more and more students want to take their exams in a private room at the Counseling Center. This creates a big hassle for the professor because that student's test paper is now separated from all the others. As a professor, I really dislike this because I write all my test questions on the whiteboard. I do this to prevent students from archiving my old exams and using them as study guides. The reasonable accommodation I provide for these students is to allow them to take their tests in our department conference room. It has windows, and the LED lights that flicker can be turned off.

Students need to be taught to ask for a specific accommodation that helps with a specific problem, rather than a blanket request such as taking all quizzes and exams at the Counseling Center.

I have also talked to several professionals who work in the field of getting people on the spectrum employed. They share my concerns. One professional told me that at one college, autistic students were given less homework. I was never given less homework. A better alternative would be to take a lighter course load and go to college for an extra year. This has worked well for many AS students.

When an individual with autism graduates and gets out into the world of employment, it is often much wiser not to fully disclose. This is especially important for the really smart, nerdy autistic kids. I received an email from a talented professional who was successfully employed for several years. He lost his job after he told his employer he had been diagnosed with autism. It was discrimination, and it was totally wrong. He needed no specific accommodation, and disclosure opened the door to blatant discrimination. Often it is better to ask for a specific accommodation instead, such as having an office cube near a window to avoid flickering LED lights. Other examples of problems and solutions include the following:

- Difficulty with remembering long strings of verbal instruction. Tell the boss you prefer emailed instructions. For tasks that require a sequence of steps, make a pilot's checklist. Checklists would help many autistic individuals keep their jobs. If the boss objects, you can say, "Pilots need a checklist, and I need one too."

- Difficulty with rapid multi-tasking, such as a busy restaurant take-out window. Try to avoid these jobs if possible, or explain, "I'm not good at rapid multi-tasking." Show your boss all the things you are really good at when you are not forced to multi-task.

- Need clear work objectives. Learn to ask lots of questions. I learned this in my design business. In order to achieve specific design objectives, I questioned the client extensively about the cattle-handling tasks he had to do in the corral. However, I never asked a client how he wanted a project designed. That was my job.

I am concerned that some individuals with autism are getting a "handicapped mentality," and think autism renders them incapable of doing and achieving certain things. Or they feel their autism diagnosis is a way out of doing the hard work that is required in life. This attitude will certainly hold them back from personal and professional success. In essence, they feel "less than"—which is not true. They are different from but not less than others. Reasonable accommodations exist to help an individual through tough spots. They aren't an excuse not to apply yourself in earnest to the tasks we all encounter in creating a life and a place for ourselves in the world.

GET OUT AND EXPERIENCE LIFE!

I am seeing too many kids and young adults on the spectrum who are not getting out and doing things. They have turned into recluses who do not want to come out of their rooms. I was absolutely not allowed to do this. I had horrible anxiety attacks, but I still had to participate in activities at both school and home.

When I went away to boarding school at age fourteen, Mr. Patey, the headmaster at Hampshire Country School, had really good instincts on when to back off and let me do my own thing and when to insist on participation. When I became interested in taking care of cleaning stalls in the horse barn, this was encouraged because I was learning work skills. I was even given insulated boots so my feet would not freeze in the winter.

Mr. Patey drew one important line in the sand. He did not let me become a recluse in my room. I had to attend all meals and classes. He also insisted that I be on time. Every Sunday I had to dress appropriately for chapel and was required to attend. When I got really anxious and did not want to attend the campus movie night, he made me the projectionist. I had to participate with the school community.

Good and Bad Accommodations

Accommodations such as a quiet environment for study and extra time on tests are really helpful. But it is important to avoid accommodations that will reinforce a victim mentality. An example of a bad accommodation is allowing a student to do a public speaking assignment over the internet. When I did my first public speaking in graduate school, I panicked and walked out. After that, I learned to use good audiovisual aids to give me cues and to prevent me from freezing up. When I did my first cattle-handling talks, I brought lots of pictures that illustrated behavioral principles. Creating excellent slides compensated for my early weak public speaking skills.

I often get asked about homeschooling. For some kids, this is a good option, but there must be lots of opportunities for social interaction with other children. I was teased and bullied and had to leave a large regular high school. For some teenagers, finishing high school online would be the right thing to do. If you choose this option, the teenager must have opportunities to interact with peers and adults through activities, volunteer work, and job experience. Teens *must* learn work skills and how to cooperate in a work environment.

Trying New Things

For individuals on the spectrum to develop, they need to be "stretched" to try new things. When I was fifteen, I was afraid to go to my aunt's ranch. I really didn't want to go! Mother gave me a choice of going for either a week or all summer. When I got out to the ranch, I loved it and chose to stay all summer. I never would have known how much I loved working on a ranch if I had not given this experience a chance.

Developing Independence

Another problem I am observing is too many kids on the high end of the spectrum who are being overprotected and coddled. They are not learning how to independently perform tasks such as shopping, ordering food in restaurants, and practicing decent hygiene. Parents and teachers can encourage independence by taking kids out into the community. At first, the child should be accompanied by an adult while shopping or going on the bus. After a few trips, they can do it by themselves.

Weighing Likes and Dislikes

There are individuals with autism who get good jobs and then quit because they "don't like it." I have seen people on the spectrum leave good jobs with sympathetic bosses because they did not want to work. A vital lesson one has to learn is that you sometimes have to do stuff you don't like. I like my work as an animal science professor, but there are some tasks that are not fun. A good job has more tasks you like than tasks you hate. A person on the spectrum needs to learn that if they have a job where they are treated decently but do not like the work, they should stick with it long enough to get a good recommendation for the next job.

Encourage your child to try new things, go new places, and develop new skills. Provide a variety of life experiences for your child as they grow. Allow your child to stretch beyond their comfort zone and relish the adventure!

CAN MY ADOLESCENT DRIVE A CAR?

Many parents ask me about the ability of people on the autism spectrum to drive a car. I have been driving since I was eighteen. I learned on the dirt roads at my aunt's ranch.

Every day for an entire summer, I drove her old pickup truck three miles to the mailbox and back, which added up to two hundred miles of driving. The truck had a manual gear shift, and it would stall unless the clutch was worked just right. Because of the difficult clutch, for the first few weeks my aunt operated the clutch and I sat beside her, learning to steer. After I learned steering, it took me several weeks to master the clutch. Aunt Ann made sure I had completely mastered steering, braking, and changing gears before she let me drive the truck on a paved road with traffic.

The main difference between a typical adolescent and a person with autism is that more time may be required to master the skills involved in driving a car, and these skills may need to be learned one piece at a time. For instance, I didn't drive on a freeway until I was completely comfortable with slower traffic. The several months of driving in the safe dirt roads on the farm provided the extra time I needed to learn safely.

Studies have shown that young adults with autism perform more poorly in a driving simulator. To help improve these poor skills, the first step I recommend is practice. Practice operating the car in a big, safe place, such as a deserted parking lot or an open field.

When a motor skill, such as driving, is being learned, all people have to consciously think about the parts involved, such as steering or operating the clutch. During this phase of motor learning, the brain's frontal cortex is very active. When a skill such as driving or steering is fully learned, the person no longer has to think about performing the sequential steps involved. Steering the car becomes automatic, and conscious thinking about how to do it is no longer required. At this point, the frontal cortex and other higher cortical regions are no longer activated. The subcortical region takes over when a skill is fully learned, and the skill is executed unconsciously. Brain imaging studies conducted by researchers at the University of Oxford clearly showed how the brain switches to lower-level systems when a complex visual and motor task is fully learned.

I would recommend that the process of steering, braking, and otherwise operating a car be fully learned to the "motor automatic" stage before permitting your son or daughter to drive in any amount of traffic or on a freeway. This helps solve the multi-tasking requirements involved with driving and frees up the frontal cortex to concentrate on traffic, rather than the operation of the car itself. When the individual first starts learning to drive, find some really safe places to practice, such as empty parking lots, open fields, or small country roads. One family had their child practice at an old closed military base.

If a child can ride a bike safely and reliably obey the traffic rules, he or she can probably drive a car. When I was ten years old, I rode my bike everywhere and always obeyed the rules.

Likewise, to be able to drive a car, a person must already know how to steer a bike, golf cart, trike, electric wheelchair, or toy vehicle. Parents interested in teaching their child to drive a car can plan ahead while the child is still young, making sure they first master some of these skills on other types of vehicles. Do not get discouraged by students that show poor driving skills. Remember, baseline skills must be learned *before* extensive driving practice is started. Performance will improve after lots of practice driving.

Another critical issue to consider is the maturity level of the individual. Does the boy or girl have enough mature judgment to drive a car? Are they careful to obey the rules given to them? How do they react under pressure? These factors need to be assessed on a case-by-case basis to determine if an adolescent is ready to tackle driving a car. I recommend allowing the person on the spectrum extra time to learn the basic operation of the car and the individual skills involved in driving. After each driving skill becomes fully learned and integrated with the other skills, they can slowly progress to driving on roads with more and more traffic, higher speeds, more frequent stops, or areas where there is a greater chance for different events to occur (for instance, driving in neighborhoods with lots of children or a high concentration of business establishments with cars pulling in and out of parking spaces regularly). Finally, nighttime driving should be avoided until the adolescent is very comfortable with all aspects of daytime driving.

I think rather than pondering, "Can my child with autism drive a car," the more appropriate question is, "Is my child ready to drive a car?" The act of driving a car can be broken down into small, manageable pieces for instruction. The motor skills can be taught and, with enough practice, can be learned. However, driving is a serious matter, one that involves more than just learned skills. Each parent needs to decide whether or not their son or daughter has the maturity and good judgment required to allow them to get behind the wheel of a car. In this regard, the parents' decision is no different for a person on the spectrum than it would be for a typical child.

A new study shows that autistic individuals who learn to drive have safety records similar to those of normal drivers. Driver's educational programs often put the individual with autism onto roads with traffic too quickly. I recommend using one tank of gas and practicing driving in a totally safe place, such as back roads, empty parking lots, or open fields. This will give the individual time to learn to operate the car before taking driver's education.

Additional Reading

Classen, S., Monahan, M., Hernandez, S. 2013. Indications of simulated driving skills in adolescents with autism spectrum disorder. *The Open Journal of Occupational Therapy* 1(4):2.

Curry, A. 2015. Driver licensing trajectories and motor vehicle crash rates among adolescents with autism spectrum disorders. American Public Health Association, online program 330458

Floyer, L.A. and Matthews, P.M. 2004. Changing brain networks for vasomotor control with increased movement automaticity. *Journal of Neuropsychology* 92:2405-2412.

Reimer, R., et al. 2013. Brief report: examining driving behavior in young adults with high functioning autism spectrum disorders: a pilot study using a driving simulation paradigm. *Journal of Autism and Developmental Disorders* 43:2211-2217.

People with autism should learn that even "normal" people have problems at work that cause stress and must be resolved.

INNOVATIVE THINKING PAVES THE WAY FOR AS CAREER SUCCESS

There are several different avenues into the workforce. The first is doing conventional interviews, which is often hard for people on the spectrum. For many autistic people, going in the back door is successful. When I started in the cattle industry, I walked up to the editor of our state farm magazine and got his card. I knew if I wrote for the magazine, it would help my career. I wrote a good article and then became livestock editor. Connections to good jobs can often be found through neighbors, coworkers, and friends. However, many people do not see the back door to jobs, and some people are too scared to "ask for the card." I saw the editor at a cattle event and just walked up to him.

Some other options for jobs are businesses that make an extra effort to hire autistic people. Some examples are Aspiritech and Walgreens. At Aspiritech, the employees test software and electric devices such as headphones. They need to find out if the headphones will work with every device. Many autistic people who are partially verbal have been successful working at coffee shops and restaurants. I have talked to many innovative people who run these businesses. The biggest problem is transportation because many autistic people do not drive. This is especially a problem in rural areas.

I have observed that the best places have a manager who really wants to make the program successful. I have seen programs that were good but became bad because management changed. The top manager sets the standards. Every successful program needs a full-time champion.

Thorkil Sonne, the father of a child with autism, has founded a business in Denmark called Specialisterne Corporation that employs AS individuals to test new computer programs. Their job is to debug new software, and their clients include Cryptomathic, a company that verifies digital signatures, and Case TDC, a major European telephone company. Testing new software is an ideal job for people with autism because the qualities of a good tester are some of the inherent strengths of a person with autism. People with autism have great memories, pay attention to details, are persistent and focused, and love structure.

Thorkil has created an innovative environment that is a win-win solution for both the employees and the corporation's clients. Because all the production employees have some degree of autism, on-the-job stress is reduced dramatically at Specialisterne Corporation. To further avoid daily stress and anxiety, work schedules are planned in advance. All tasks have well-defined goals, and they are agreed upon in advance. Specialisterne will hire and train qualified job applicants that have autism. He uses the Lego Mindstorms programmable robots as a testing tool. That way, job applicants can demonstrate their programming skills with the robots instead of going through a formal interview process.

There are two things that Specialisterne does not tolerate: (1) anger where equipment is damaged or other people are hit, and (2) an individual who constantly stirs up gossip and conflict between coworkers. In return, the Aspies are provided with a work environment where sensory distractions are minimized and they do not have to deal with difficult bosses and complex social situations.

Today, Specialisterne has three European offices and employs fifty-plus individuals, three-quarters of whom are on the autism spectrum, to work with corporate clients. Major software companies such as SAP are now actively seeking people with autism because they have skills that are superior for debugging software.

AS-IT in Lincolnshire, England, is another organization working with individuals with autism, in this case to train them for information technology positions in large corporations. The "coaching" structure of AS-IT helps prevent problems with bosses who do not understand the employee with autism. When a corporation hires one of AS-IT's trainees, the trainee can stay in contact with AS-IT for assistance in the job transition as needed. Because the corporation knows they will be getting an employee with autism and has increased awareness about autism through their partnership with AS-IT, they are able to help avoid misunderstandings when social situations develop that might have previously resulted in an individual with autism being fired.

Over the years I have observed that the two main reasons a successful long-term autistic employee was fired are because of (1) a new, unsympathetic boss and (2) the employee with autism was promoted into a job that involved complex social skills and social interaction. The person may have been outstanding in a technical position, such as draftsman, engineer, or programmer, and they failed when promoted into a management position.

Employers need to be informed that promotion into management is not the best career path for individuals with autism and many technical-type people. These two corporations are using innovative thinking to design work environments in which people with autism can flourish.

The individuals with autism find the support they need to be successful, and the corporations find brilliant minds that can propel their businesses forward. Win-win solutions like this are possible when neurotypicals start thinking outside the box and value the positive contributions individuals have to offer.

Another approach to getting people with autism employed is to create a company composed of people with autism that do not advertise that they have autism. I visited a successful animation company that used this approach. They found a niche business, which the big animation companies had been farming out to other countries. Now, instead of sending animation work such as movie titles and screen shading to India, clients are hiring these folks in the United States.

Another wide-open area is the skilled trades. Today, there is a huge shortage of automotive mechanics, machinists, plumbers, electrical utility workers, certified welders for the oil industry, and many others. Skilled trades are fields that will appeal to many visual and mathematical thinkers, and these jobs will never be outsourced to another country. Another advantage of these jobs is that they will not be taken over by artificial intelligence.

Additional Reading

D'eri, T. (2023) *The Power of Potential*, Harper Collins, New York.

Grandin, T. (2022) *Visual Thinking: The Hidden Gifts of People Who Think in Pictures, Patterns, and Abstractions.*

Miller-Merrell, J. (2016) Twenty-seven companies who have adults with autism, Workology.com.

Putterman, L.C. (2023) How Walgreens prospers hiring people with disabilities, larryputterman.com

Wang, S. 2014. How autism can help you land a job. *The Wall Street Journal* Business Section, March 27, 2014.

TRY ON CAREERS

For all students, it is important to find a career they will like. I get asked all the time, "How did you get interested in the cattle industry?" I came from a nonagricultural background and became interested in the cattle industry when I visited my aunt's ranch at age fifteen. Students get interested in things they get exposed to. A big problem for many students on the autism spectrum is that they do not get exposed to enough new things. When a student is in both high school and college, they need to get employment in real jobs outside the home. The first job in high school teaches job skills, and internships during college or apprenticeships let a student explore different careers.

Parents are often reluctant to get their child with autism out into the world. They are afraid that the child may become too anxious. When a teenager with autism finally gets out doing a job, they often blossom and love it. Some jobs where teens with autism have excelled are office supply stores, bagging groceries, and ice cream shops. In these jobs, the pace is slower and the teen can learn how to interact with customers. Since multi-tasking is often difficult, a super-busy fast-food restaurant may be too hard. A busy store during the holiday season would be another poor choice.

A common mistake made by parents, teachers, or vocational counselors is that they do not differentiate between an individual for which bagging groceries is a temporary training job and a more intellectually challenged person for which it is an appropriate career. Research has shown that students on the spectrum who successfully keep jobs before they graduate are often more successful in the workplace. Getting and keeping jobs before graduation provides a gradual transition from the academic world to successful employment.

Opportunities for Individuals with Autism in Skilled Trades

Today there is a big shortage of people in the high-end skilled trades, such as electricians, plumbers, welders who can build things from blueprints, mechanics, and heat and air conditioning technicians. These are good careers that will never get replaced by computers. I spent most of my career working with talented skilled tradespeople who built the livestock facilities that I designed. Many of these talented people were dyslexic or socially awkward. If these individuals had been children today, they would be in the special education department with an autism diagnosis. The people I worked with are now either retiring or getting ready to retire. They are not getting replaced. Due to the lack of new people entering the skilled trades, the US is losing the skills to build industrial equipment. Equipment that is essential for industries such as automated meat warehouses and food packaging, now has to be imported at great expense. We do not make it anymore. There are many individuals who might love a skilled trade. They will not know until they try it.

Introduce Students to Tools

The problem is that kids are growing up without using tools. I have observed talented sixteen-year-olds who are still building with Legos because tools were never introduced. Removing hands-on skilled trades classes from the schools was a huge mistake. There are a few progressive school districts that are putting these classes back in. Those with my kind of mind, the visual thinkers, are often a perfect fit for skilled trades. There are kids who can build anything but cannot do algebra. Algebra is not needed for skilled trades. It must be removed as a barrier to the trades. A person who is really good at a highly skilled trade can have a job they will love for the rest of their career. The pay is good and there are full health benefits.

Research shows that there is a difference between an object visualizer, like me, who thinks in photo-realistic pictures, and a mathematical visual-spatial thinker who thinks in patterns. The third type is the verbal thinker, who thinks in words. The object visualizers would be good at skilled trades, art, animals, photography, and anything mechanical. The math minds would be good at computer programming, chemistry, physics, music, and data analytics. The autistic word thinker who can memorize many facts and figures has been successful in jobs where knowledge of the merchandise is appreciated. Autistic people have thrived selling things like new cars, sporting goods, specialized financial products, office supplies, and auto parts.

College Students on the Spectrum Should Do Summer Internships When They Are in College

Each summer when a student is in college, they should do a different internship. This will enable them to try on careers and find out what they like. It is also equally important to find out what they hate. In the Animal Science Department at Colorado State University, we have many undergraduates who came from a nonagricultural background. They often get recruited to assist with research projects in the beef industry. When these nonagricultural students experience working on a research project in either a large feedlot or meat plant, we discover that two usually love it and one hates it. A student will not find out what they love or hate until they try it.

Today all students are encouraged to do internships when they are in college. Typical internships are designed to teach students how to solve problems and enable them to get to know a possible future employer. Interns no longer do menial work or just observe. They are usually assigned a real problem that they have to solve. Some examples of actual problems they had to solve during meat industry internships were: why was the automated warehouse losing boxes of meat? Or, what is the optimal speed at which to run a chicken wing processing line to get both efficiency and quality? An engineering student had to figure out why the electric forklifts were frequently running out of battery charge. After calling the company that made the forklifts, he learned that they were using the wrong charger. Students who can jump right in and solve these real problems will get hired.

The student also has to observe and learn how to work with other people to solve the problem. Some of these problems required an entire summer to solve. Not all internships involve factories. There are also internships at banks, insurance companies, and hospitals.

Of high school students with autism who did Project SEARCH job internships, 73 percent were employed after high school. In controls with no internships, only 17 percent were employed after high school. In the future, what will artificial intelligence do to jobs? Hands-on jobs will be safe, such as skilled trades, nursing, live theater, and service jobs. AI is most likely to replace many people in computer programming, cartoon animation, video game design, and medical diagnostics.

Additional Reading

Adler, A.L. (2018) Chronic shortage of service techs threatens dealership profits, *Automotive News*, August 20, 2018.

Grandin, T. (2022) *Visual Thinking: The Hidden Gifts of People Who Think in Pictures, Patterns, and Abstractions*, Penguin Random House, New York.

Gross, A. and Marus, J. (2018) High paying trade jobs sit empty, while high school graduates line up for university, *All Things Considered*, National Public Radio.

Kozhevnikov, M. et al. (2002) Revising the visualizer-verbalizer dimensions: Evidence for two types of visualizers, *Cognition and Instruction*, 20(1):47-77.

Kozhevnikov, M. et al. (2005) Spatial verses object visualizers: A new characterization of visual cognitive style, *Memory and Cognition*, 33(4):710-726.

Vopini, M. (2018) People with autism can help fill U.S. shortage of stem workers, *Dallas News*, February 7, 2018.

Wehman, P. et al. (2019) Competitive employment for transition age youth with significant impact with autism: A multi-site randomized clinical trial, *Journal of Autism and Developmental Disorders*.

The way I see it, it is likely that the genetics that produce autism are the same genetics that create an Einstein or a Mozart—it is more a matter of degree.

THE LINK BETWEEN AUTISM GENETICS AND GENIUS

As a society, we still tend to view disabilities in a negative light. We may use politically correct language and say these people are "challenged" or "differently abled," but the fact remains that we generally focus more on what they can't do and tend to overlook the positive traits many of these individuals possess. Such is the case with people with autism. If the genetic factors that cause autism were eliminated from the human race, we would pay a terrible price. The way I see it, it is likely that the genetics that produce autism are the same genetics that create an Einstein or a Mozart—it is more a matter of degree. A little of the genetic expression produces highly creative, brilliant thinkers. Too much of the genetics, however, results in severe autism, a nonverbal and much more challenged child.

If Albert Einstein were born today, he would be diagnosed with autism. He had no speech until age three, obsessively repeated certain sentences until the age of seven, and spent hours building houses from playing cards. His social skills remained odd through most of his life, and he was a self-described loner:

> My passionate sense of social justice and social responsibility has always contrasted oddly with my pronounced lack of need for direct contact with other human beings and

human communities. I am truly a lone traveler and have never belonged to my country, my home, my friends, or even my immediate family, with my whole heart. In the face of all these ties, I have never lost a sense of distance and a need for solitude.

— Albert Einstein, 1954

A host of other brilliant historic figures, such as Isaac Newton, Thomas Jefferson, Socrates, Lewis Carroll, Glenn Gould, and Andy Warhol, are now speculated to have been on the autism spectrum.

Several books have been written that profile famous scientists, musicians, and artists who were on the autism/Asperger's spectrum. In his 2007 release, *Genius Genes: How Asperger Talents Changed the World*, Michael Fitzgerald, professor of psychiatry at Trinity College, Dublin, reached the conclusion that autism, creativity, and genius were all caused by similar genes, after comparing the characteristics of more than 1,600 people he had diagnosed with known biographical details of famous people. I see it the same way: A mild case of autism and being eccentric are the *same* thing, and the positive characteristics of being on the autism spectrum—detailed thinking, unwavering focus, obsessive interest in certain topics—are the very qualities that result in genius thought and world-changing discoveries. Simon-Baron Cohen, a researcher at the University of Cambridge, England, found that within families of children with autism, there existed a significantly greater number of parents and/or close relatives working as engineers and other technical professionals. In my family, my grandfather was an MIT-trained engineer who was coinventor of the automatic pilot for airplanes.

Geeks, nerds, and eccentrics have always been in the world; what has changed is the world itself and our expectations of others within it. I work in a technical field and have worked with many engineers and other technical people who definitely displayed marked characteristics of autism. Most of these people are now in their forties, fifties, and sixties—and they are all undiagnosed. They were brought up in an era where social rules were more strictly defined and were carefully taught to all children. This more rigid upbringing actually helped these children acquire enough social skills to get by in the world. Many are successful, and they have held good jobs for years. I know one meat plant engineer with autism who keeps a multimillion-dollar plant running.

I get worried that today an autism diagnosis may be detrimental to some individuals and hold them back. With greater competition for a shrinking number of jobs, a person's social capabilities are now looked at as closely as the person's technical skills or intellectual abilities. The most successful people with mild autism work in places such as Silicon Valley, where superior talent still trumps social skills. Often these individuals have parents who are also in a high-tech field, and as the child grew, they placed more importance on teaching their children computer programming and other technical skills than worrying about whether or not they had girlfriends or boyfriends or wanted to attend every school dance.

I have given talks at conferences geared to a number of different diagnostic categories, such as autism, gifted, and dyslexia. Even though diagnosis is not precise, each diagnostic group lives in its own world. When I go to the book tables, there are very few books stocked on *both* an autism book table and a gifted book table. The books addressing these individuals may be different, but I see the same bright kids at both autism and gifted children meetings. The autism child at the gifted meeting is doing well in school, but the child at an autism meeting may be in a poor special ed program, bored, and getting into trouble because adults in his life hold lower expectations of his abilities. Unfortunately, in some cases, people are so hung up on the labels attached to students that they teach to these low expectations and aren't even curious to learn if the child is actually more capable. This is mostly likely to occur when the label is *autism* instead of *gifted but developmentally delayed*.

Parents and teachers should look at the child, not the child's label, and remember that the same genes that produce his autism may have given the child the capacity to become one of the truly great minds of his generation. Be realistic with expectations, but don't overlook the potential for genius that may be quietly hiding inside, just waiting for an opportunity to express itself.

Additional Reading

Baron-Cohen, S. 2000. Is Asperger syndrome/high functioning autism necessarily a disability? *Developmental Psychopathology* 12: 480-500.

Baron-Cohen, S., et al. 2007. Mathematical talent is linked to autism. *Human Nature* 18:125-131.

Einstein, A. 1954. *The World As I See It. In Ideas and Opinions, Based on Mein Weltbild.* Carl Seelig, editor. New York: Bonanza Books, pp. 8-11.

Fitzgerald, M., and B. O'Brien. 2007. *Genius Genes: How Asperger Talents Changed the World.* Shawnee Mission, KS: Autism Asperger Publishing Company.

Grandin, T. 2006. *Thinking in Pictures* (Expanded Edition). New York: Vintage/Random House.

Grandin, T. (2022) *Visual Thinking: The Hidden Gifts of People Who Think in Pictures, Patterns, and Abstractions*, Penguin Random House, New York.

Ledgin, N. 2002. *Aspergers and Self-Esteem: Insight and Hope through Famous Role Models*. Arlington, TX: Future Horizons, Inc. (This book profiles famous scientists and musicians who probably had Asperger's.)

Lyons, V., and Fitzgerald, M. 2013. Critical evaluation of the concept of autistic creativity. *Intech.* http://dx.doi. org/5772/54465

Soullieves, I. 2011. Enhanced mental image mapping in autism. *Neuropsychologia* 49:848-857.

Stevenson, J.L., and Gernsbacher, M.A. 2013. Abstract spatial reasoning on autistic strength. *PLOS One*. DOI: 10 1371/ journal. pone.0059329 .

MY SENSE OF SELF-IDENTITY

One of my big concerns today is that too many children and teens on the autism spectrum are identifying so much with autism that it is hindering their pathway to success. When I was a teenager, I was fixated on science, horses, and the projects I built. These fixations were the basis of my self-identity and helped propel me into a successful career. Today, I am seeing smart individuals who have become so fixated on "their autism" that their entire lives revolve around it. When I was young, I talked endlessly about my favorite activities instead of autism. My fixations motivated me to create projects such as gates, horse bridles, carpentry work, and signs, which were all things other people wanted and appreciated. While creating these projects, I was also doing activities with other people. Teachers and parents need to work with both children and adults to get them involved in activities where they can have shared interests with other people, such as choir, art, auto mechanics, karate, working with animals, robot club, or drama club.

I have given several talks at large technical and computer conferences. At these conferences, I see lots of undiagnosed adults on the autism spectrum who have successful, high-level careers. All they talk about is the latest computer stuff; social chitchat bores them. Then the next day I travel to an autism conference, and I meet a smart teenager who only wants to talk about autism. I would rather talk to him about an intense interest such as art, astronomy, history, or computers. It is fine to talk about autism, but it should not be the primary focus of an individual's life. Autism support groups are excellent because they enable individuals on the spectrum to communicate with others who have the same challenges. It is comforting for them to find out that they are not the only ones who are different.

However, there should be other activities so that the person's life does not totally center on autism. Parents are pivotal in making this happen in a child's life. Several adults on the spectrum have talked to me about their autism-centric lives. They were either unemployed or had a boring, low-level job such as stocking shelves. I encouraged one of them to start a tutoring service and another to find activities involving music. They needed some activities that had nothing to do with autism. I will never forget an autistic individual who wanted to interview me about autism. He seemed kind of depressed. When I got him off the subject of autism, he got really happy and excited when he told me about the sports photography he had done for a major sports network. I suggested that he pursue sports photography, and he is loving it. His career has become really successful. On the other hand, I have talked to older adults on the spectrum who had successful, high-level careers, but in their personal lives, they felt empty. These individuals can greatly benefit from an autism support group.

At this stage in my adult life, being a college professor in the livestock industry is my primary identity, and autism is secondary. Autism is an important part of me, and I like my autistic, logical way of thinking. I would never want to be cured and made "normal." To have a satisfying life, I do many things that have nothing to do with autism. The most successful people on the autism spectrum have either a career or activities they love to do. The nerds and the geeks at the computer conference were all kind of eccentric. Many were dressed in layered T-shirts like Sheldon wears in the television series *The Big Bang Theory*. Being eccentric is OK. I am kind of eccentric with my Western clothes. In the HBO movie based on my life, there is a scene where a can of deodorant is slammed on the table and my boss says, "Use it, you stink."

That actually happened, and today I thank my boss. It is fine to be eccentric, but being dirty is not acceptable. There are too many teenagers and adults showing up in public unshaven or in messy clothes. I encourage people on the spectrum to be unique, but they should be neat. I met one man who taught college astronomy, and he had a long ponytail and a cool astronomy T-shirt. I told him, "Don't let anybody tell you to cut your ponytail. Be a proud geek who can excel in an interesting career."

Now that I'm seventy-six, looking back on my life, I remember how I spent a lot of time during my twenties trying to figure out the ultimate meaning of life. I suppose that is not very different from other young adults at that age as we try to define ourselves and find our own way. Today I find meaning in doing things that make real, positive changes in the world. When a mother tells me that reading my book helped her understand her child, or when a rancher tells me that the corrals I designed work well, that provides meaning to my life.

Did you like this book?

Rate it and share your opinion!

BARNES&NOBLE
BOOKSELLERS
www.bn.com

amazon.com

Not what you expected? Tell us!

Most negative reviews occur when the book did not reach expectation. Did the description build any expectations that were not met? Let us know how we can do better.

Please drop us a line at info@fhautism.com.
Thank you so much for your support!

FUTURE HORIZONS

Printed in the USA
CPSIA information can be obtained
at www.ICGtesting.com
JSHW011559160924
69913JS00009B/15